Kampuchea
Between
China and Vietnam

Kampuchea
Between
China and Vietnam

CHANG PAO-MIN

SINGAPORE UNIVERSITY PRESS
NATIONAL UNIVERSITY OF SINGAPORE

© 1985 Singapore University Press
Kent Ridge, Singapore 0511

Reprint 1987

ISBN 9971-69-089-6 (Paper)

DS
554.8
C44
1985

Typeset by : Art Communication Workshop
Printed by : Chong Moh Offset Printing Pte. Ltd.

iv

CONTENTS

ACKNOWLEDGMENTS   vii

ABBREVIATIONS   ix

INTRODUCTION   xi

1. Kampuchea in Chinese and Vietnamese Policies 1
2. The Precarious Triangular Alliance 27
3. Towards Open Conflict 51
4. The Double Invasions 72
5. Between Peace and War 91
6. Beijing's Diplomacy 113
7. Hanoi's Diplomacy 134
8. Kampuchea and Sino-Vietnamese Relations 157

APPENDICES

1. Treaty of Friendship and Mutual Non-Aggression
   Between the People's Republic of China and
   the Kingdom of Cambodia 181
2. Treaty of Friendship and Cooperation Between the
   Socialist Republic of Vietnam and the Lao
   People's Democratic Republic 184
3. Treaty of Friendship and Cooperation Between the
   Socialist Republic of Vietnam and the
   Union of Soviet Socialist Republics 189
4. Treaty of Peace, Friendship and Cooperation Between
   the Socialist Republic of Vietnam and the People's
   Republic of Kampuchea 194
5. Agreement on Economic, Cultural, Scientific and
   Technological Cooperation Between the Lao People's
   Democratic Republic and the People's Republic of
   Kampuchea 199

INDEX   201

ACKNOWLEDGMENTS

The author wishes to acknowledge the financial support he received in the course of preparing this study from the National University of Singapore. He is also grateful to the publishers of *Asian Survey, International Affairs, Studies in Comparative Communism,* and *Survey* for their permission to reproduce materials written by him which have appeared earlier in these publications.

ABBREVIATIONS

BR	Beijing Review (Beijing)
FEER	Far Eastern Economic Review (Hong Kong)
MD	The Monitoring Digest (Singapore)
RH	Radio Hanoi (Hanoi)
ST	The Straits Times (Singapore)
VNA	Vietnam News Agency (Hanoi)
XHNA	Xinhua News Agency (Beijing)

INTRODUCTION

That the Kampuchean issue has been a source of bitter conflict between China and Vietnam is quite clear to all. What is puzzling and perhaps debatable is the reason why the two communist rivals should have become so intensely entangled in the affairs of a third nation, and the extent to which both have been prepared to go in order to defend their interests in that country. Coming after the territorial dispute and following almost immediately the ethnic controversy, the conflict over Kampuchea represents the climax of the Sino-Vietnamese split and also renders the other two disputes insolvable. With an immediate impact upon the security of the entire region, it also assumes a dimension not amenable to the control of either side. So far the Vietnamese have consistently maintained that they went into Kampuchea and have remained there in order to meet China's threat, whereas the Chinese have claimed that they intervened only to prevent the annexation of the country by Vietnam. Whatever the validity of the charges and counter-charges, the war continues. What after all have been the respective objectives of the two countries in Kampuchea? How did the conflict begin and evolve? And what are the prospects of a negotiated settlement of this Third Indochina War? This book seeks to answer some of these questions.

1
Kampuchea in Chinese and Vietnamese Policies

Like the territorial and ethnic disputes between China and Vietnam, the conflict over Kampuchea is rooted in the past and cannot be separated from the broader geopolitical rivalry between China and the Soviet Union. Unlike them, however, the dispute did not arise from issues immediately affecting the sovereign rights of the two countries, but can be traced, at least in part, to a fundamental difference between China and Vietnam in their perceptions of the status of Kampuchea that have been shaped by geography and history. Nearly six hundred miles from the Chinese border and all but entirely enclosed by other Southeast Asian nations, Kampuchea until the middle of the twentieth century was marginal to China's concerns and never a target of Chinese political influence. In fact, Kampuchea is the only country in mainland Southeast Asia which has never witnessed Chinese military intervention or been subjugated by China, even at the zenith of the imperial power during the Yuan Dynasty.[1] Being culturally the single most Indianized nation in the region,[2] Kampuchea was also conspicuously outside the periphery of Chinese civilization throughout her history. As such she has always been recorded and described by the Chinese

---

1. Huang Xionglue, *Jianpuzai zhilue* (A Short Survey of Kampuchea) (Shanghai: Zhengzhong shuju, 1947), pp. 27–33. See also, Martin F. Herz, *A Short History of Cambodia* (New York: Praeger, 1958), pp. 39–55.
2. Brian Harrison, *Southeast Asia: A Short History* (London: MacMillan, 1967), pp. 21–23. Herz, *op. cit.*, pp. 7–10.

as a separate nation with its distinct culture and ethnic peculiarities.[3] Consequently, although Sino-Kampuchean relations date back to the third century A.D. and Kampuchea did send tribute-bearing missions to China during the ensuing millennium or so, such contacts were most irregular and perfunctory and were maintained only insofar as the Khmer Empire showed any interest in China.[4] Yet even at the peak of development of China's tributary relations with the Southeast Asian countries in the early fifteenth century, Kampuchea stood out in Chinese records as the country which attracted the least attention from China in the entire region.[5] And at least twice in history, i.e., in A.D. 1200 and again in A.D.1374, the imperial court decreed that Kampuchea should dispense with the tribute-

---

3. Li Changfu, *Zhongguo zhimin shi* (A History of Chinese Emmigration) (Shanghai: Shangwu shuju, 1946), pp. 74, 101, 102, 105, 117. Zhao Lingyang, *et al.* (ed.), *Southeast Asia in Chinese Reign Chronicles, 1368-1644* (Hong Kong: Xuejing Press, 1976), p. 16ff. The only extensive written account of Kampuchea in the Chinese language before the twentieth century was a travelogue compiled towards the end of the thirteenth century by a Chinese scholar-official named Zhou Daguan, who visited the country as a member of a Mongol embassy. The book was for centuries considered as the only authoritative source of reference, yet it gave every impression that Kampuchea was a strange land with few similarities to China. See Zhou Daguan, *Zhengla fongtu ji* (The Land and People of Kampuchea) (Shanghai: Zhonghua shuju, 1934).

4. Huang Xionglue, *op. cit.*, pp. 27-33. Also, D.G.E. Hall, *A History of Southeast Asia* (London: MacMillan Co., 3rd edition, 1976), pp. 95-96.

5. Among all Southeast Asian states, including Brunei, Kampuchea received the fewest missions from China and also sent the fewest to China. See Wang Gungwu, "Early Ming Relations with Southeast Asia: A Background Essay", in John K. Fairbank (ed.), *The Chinese World Order* (Cambridge, Mass.: Harvard University Press, 1968), p. 58.

paying practice due to the long distance involved and the rough journey entailed.[6]

From the mid-fifteenth century on, as a result of the steady decline of the Khmer Empire and the growing power of first Siam (Thailand) and then Vietnam, Kampuchea for more than 400 years virtually disappeared from China's court records and historical accounts.[7] While the French occupation of Kampuchea in 1862 was hardly taken note of, throughout her prolonged negotiations with France over Indochina in the late nineteenth century, China was exclusively concerned with the status and problems of Vietnam and did not raise a single question on Kampuchea which had never been part of the Chinese Empire.[8] However, neither the imperial nor the republican Chinese government considered the Indochinese Union set up by the French in 1887 as more than a loose confederation of nations, and both took note of the French-Siamese Treaty of 1867 by which France pledged never to incorporate Kampuchea into Vietnam, as well as the fact that both Kampuchea and Laos enjoyed a more or less co-equal status with the three parts of Vietnam under French domination, each retaining its separate monarchical system and administrative structure.[9] While lending considerable moral and material support to the Indochinese anti-colonial movement against France in the first

---

6. *Ibid.* Huang Xionglue, *op. cit.*, p. 30. Li Changfu, *op. cit.*, pp. 102, 117.

7. Hall, *op. cit.*, pp. 125–35.

8. This fact is evident from the numerous memorials and diplomatic correspondences on Sino-French relations. See Zhongguo shixue hui (The History Society of China) (ed.), *Zhong-Fa Zhanzheng* (The Sino-French War) (Shanghai: Renmin chubanshe, 1961), 7 volumes, particularly Vols. 5 and 6. Also, Shao Xunzheng, *Zhong-Fa Yuenan guanxi shimuo* (A History of Sino-French Relations Concerning Vietnam) (Beijing, 1935), p. 55ff.

9. Shao Xungzheng, *op. cit.*, Also, Li Changfu, *Nanyang shigang* (A Short History of Southeast Asia) (Hong Kong: Nanhua chubanshe, 1959), p. 65.

half of the twentieth century, the republican Chinese government, in particular, openly championed the cause of national self-determination for *all* the three Indochinese nations.[10] During World War II, China actually clashed with France over the future of Indochina and considered the conclusion of the war as naturally meaning the end of French rule in Indochina and the restoration of the sovereign independence of Kampuchea, Laos and Vietnam.[11] And had it not been for China's growing fear of communist activities in Vietnam and her worsening civil war, France would most probably not have been allowed to re-establish her colonial authority over Indochina in 1946.[12] Yet both before and after the withdrawal of nearly 60,000 Chinese occupation troops from Vietnam, the Chinese government repeatedly took the trouble of disclaiming any territorial ambitions in Indochina and continued to express its wishes to see the eventual full independence of all the nations in the region.[13] The establishment of the People's Republic in 1949 did not lead to any change of this basic position on Indochina. Beijing continued to see Kampuchea and Laos as separate nations fighting for their respective salvation; China was also the first communist nation to recognize North Viet-

---

10. Joseph Buttinger, *A Political History of Vietnam* (London, Andre Deutch, 1969), pp. 157–59, 198–201, 208–9, 228–29; Nguyen Khac Huyen, *Vision Accomplished?* (New York: Collier Books, 1971), pp. 57–65, 223. Also, King C. Chen, *Vietnam and China* (Princeton, N.J.: Princeton University Press, 1969), pp. 55–85ff; Chiang Kai-shek, *China's Destiny* (New York: MacMillan Co., 1947), pp. 253–60.
11. Buttinger, *op. cit.*, pp. 204, 228–29. Chen, *op. cit.*, pp. 91–92, 95–97, 112.
12. Chen, *op. cit.*, p. 98; Ellen J. Hammer, *The Struggle for Indochina: 1940–1955* (Stanford: Stanford University Press, 1954), pp. 129–34, 153. Huyen, *op. cit.*, p. 97; Buttinger, *op. cit.*, 235–41.
13. Huyen, *loc. cit.; Zhongyang Ribao* (Central Daily) (Chongqing), August 25, 1945, p. 1; March 1, 1946, p. 2; March 3, 1946, p. 3.

nam as an independent sovereign state, and one of her first diplomatic acts was to escalate her military and economic aid to the Viet Minh who were fighting for the liberation of Indochina.[14]

Vietnam's perception of and relationship to Kampuchea have been qualitatively different from China's. The destinies of the two countries have been closely tied together not only by geography but also by history. Whereas the Khmer Empire was until the late seventeenth century in control of the southern third of Vietnam, traditionally known as Cochinchina, the entire area of sparsely populated and yet agriculturally rich Mekong Delta had been the natural target of a long but steady process of southward and westward expansion of the Vietnamese after their full independence from China in the tenth century.[15] Following the conquest of the Chams — a nation occupying the central coastal region of present-day Vietnam — in the late fifteenth century, Vietnam began to challenge Kampuchea's power and penetrate into her territory.[16] As a result of their sheer numerical superiority and better organizational skills, the Vietnamese quickly gained the upper hand in the confrontation and steadily expanded their territorial control into Kampuchea.[17] Being more sophisticated as well as markedly different from the Khmers both ethnically and culturally, the Vietnamese in fact "held themselves to be superior to the other peoples of Indochina",[18] and, once in contact with the Khmers, also assumed the role of the "civilizers" by undertaking to assimilate the Khmers and displacing their institutions and

---

14. Hammer, *op. cit.*, pp. 250, 252–53, Chen, *op. cit.*, pp. 217–19, 221, 232, 260, 278. See also *Xinhua yuebao* (New China Monthly), November 1950, p. 84; December 1950, p. 565.
15. Buttinger, *op. cit.*, p. 51; Milton Osborne, "Kampuchea and Viet Nam: A Historical Perspective", *Pacific Community*, April 1978, p. 252.
16. Buttinger, *op. cit.*, pp. 41–50.
17. *Ibid.*, p. 13.
18. Hall, *op. cit.*, p. 762.

values with the Vietnamese ones.[19] In fact, from the seventeenth century on, Vietnam repeatedly intervened in Kampuchean affairs, and was consequently entangled in two centuries of diplomatic and military tussles with an equally aggressive Thailand, which sought to eclipse Kampuchea from the west.[20] As a matter of historical record, after the sixteenth century, Kampuchea paid tributes first to Thailand, and then alternatively and sometimes even simultaneously, to the Vietnamese and Siamese kingdoms, depending on their relative strength, but no longer to China.[21] However, since the Vietnamese were militarily the stronger, by the 1830s, most of lowland Kampuchea to the south and east of the Thai-controlled provinces of Battambang and Siemreap had been occupied by Vietnamese forces and administered by Vietnamese officials.[22] A large-scale Vietnamization campaign was in fact launched at the same time to transform the kingdom in all its cultural aspects.[23] The independence of the Khmer state was salvaged only by a mass rebellion against the Vietnamese occupation and with the energetic intervention of Thailand.[24] And had it not been for the French intervention, the country would have been

---

19. This explained the Khmers' traditional resentment towards the Vietnamese but not towards the culturally similar Thais who sought only to exercise their overlordship through Khmer institutions. David J. Steinberg *et al.*, *In Search of Southeast Asia: A Modern History* (Kuala Lumpur: Oxford University Press, 1975), pp. 119–20. Also, John F. Cady, *Thailand, Burma, Laos and Cambodia* (New York: Prentice-Hall, 1966), p. 114; Osborne, *op. cit.*, p. 253.
20. Hall, *op. cit.*, pp. 421–69, particularly pp. 432, 438–39, 442–43, 465, 468–69. Herz, *op. cit.*, pp. 14–28, 43–55.
21. Hall, *op. cit.*, pp. 421–69; Herz, *op. cit.*, p. 50. Also, Mark Mancell, "The Ch'ing Tribute System: An Interpretive Essay", in Fairbank, *op. cit.*, p. 68.
22. Osborne, *op. cit.*, p. 253.
23. *Ibid.*
24. *Ibid.*

successfully annexed by Vietnam in her renewed, massive advance into Kampuchea in the middle of the nineteenth century.[25]

Although France put an end to the ambitions of Vietnam in Kampuchea, the creation of a French Indochina actually lent legitimacy to the identity of the entire Indochina as a single, united political entity, by firmly enclosing Kampuchea into the union.[26] It also inevitably strengthened the traditional Vietnamese perceptions of Kampuchea by elevating Hanoi to the status of a colonial capital and therefore somewhat formalizing and perpetuating the suzerainty relationship between Vietnam on the one hand, and Laos and Kampuchea on the other.[27] The nominal separation in administrative structures and boundaries between the member states was quickly blurred by uniform policies throughout Indochina and the free flow of resources and manpower across their boundaries. Moreover, French colonial policy in Indochina clearly favoured the Vietnamese vis-à-vis the Kampucheans. It not only allowed considerable Vietnamese participation in administration but also redrew the boundaries between Vietnam and Kampuchea in such a way as to be advantageous to Vietnam.[28] In fact, the French saw Kampucheans as a "fallen race" and encouraged Vietnamese presence in Kampuchea in the form of permanent

---

25. *Ibid.*, pp. 253–54. Also, Hall, *op. cit.*, pp. 442–43.
26. Hanoi in fact did not hesitate to emphasize this historical reality. For instance, Hoang Nguyen, *The Vietnam-Kampuchea Conflict* (Hanoi: Foreign Languages Publishing House, 1979), p. 1; *Vietnam Courier*, July 1980, pp. 10–11.
27. In fact, one of the reasons why France wanted to establish a protectorate over Kampuchea was that Vietnam was a suzerain to Kampuchea and France had inherited Vietnam's rights. Milton E. Osborne, *The French Presence in Cochinchina and Cambodia* (Ithaca: Cornell University Press, 1969), pp. 31–32.
28. *Ibid.*, pp. 119–31ff. For a detailed account of the border issue, see Sarin Chhak, *Les Frontieres du Cambodge* (Paris, 1966), esp. pp. 125–30.

settlement for both political and economic purposes.[29] As a result, by the 1950s there were already 300,000 Vietnamese in Kampuchea[30] and, throughout the eighty-year French rule, the Vietnamese continued to regard the Khmers, as well as the Laotians, more as subject peoples than as peoples of different states.[31]

The special relationship between Vietnam and Kampuchea was enshrined by the development of the anti-French nationalist movement in the twentieth century. When the Indochinese Communist Party was founded in 1930, it was meant to be a united movement.[32] As a communist document of 1934 put it, "there is no place for considering Cambodian revolution on its own. There can only be an Indochinese revolution".[33] In fact, not only did the Indochinese Communist Party's platforms throughout the 1930s and 1940s stress the need for Vietnam to "unite closely" with Kampuchea and Laos, and repeatedly cite an independent Indochina or "Indochina federation" as its final goal,[34] but the entire movement from the very outset was also

---

29. Osborne, *The French Presence in Cochinchina and Cambodia*, pp. 47-49, 145-47, 202-3ff, 275-76. Also, Osborne, "Kampuchea and Vietnam", p. 254; D.J. M.Tate, *The Making of Southeast Asia* (Kuala Lumpur: Oxford University Press, 1979), Vol. II, pp. 387, 395; *FEER*, February 2, 1979, p. 18.

30. Herz, *op. cit.*, p. 71. According to Milton Osborne, there were at least half a million Vietnamese in Kampuchea by 1967. Osborne, "Kampuchea and Vietnam", p. 256.

31. Virginia Thompson, *French Indochina* (London: Allen and Unwin, Ltd., 1937), p. 485.

32. It was based on Ho Chi Minh's proposal that the three communist groups in Vietnam (i.e., North, Centre, and South) merged into a single party under the name of Communist Party of Indochina. Bernard B. Fall (ed.), *Ho Chi Minh on Revolution: Selected Writings, 1920-1966* (London: Pall Mall, 1967), pp. 127, 129.

33. Quoted in Osborne, "Kampuchea and Vietnam", p. 257. Also, Huyen, *op. cit.*, pp. 220-22.

34 *Ibid.*, pp. 141-42; Osborne, "Kampuchea and Vietnam", p. 257.

dominated and controlled by Vietnamese with little participation of ethnic Kampucheans or Laotians.[35] Although the circumstances that surrounded these developments were in accord with the reality of a single identity of all Indochinese nations and were by no means entirely under the control of the Vietnamese,[36] their net effect could not but reinforce Vietnam's traditional self-perceptions. The Vietnamese thus more or less saw themselves as natural leaders responsible for overseeing the interests and well-being of all the three peoples and considered it as a matter of course to speak for the entire Indochina and to plan for its future.[37] The prolonged armed struggle towards independence and the decisive role played by the Vietnamese communists in it only further convinced them of the interdependence of the three parts of Indochina, and the leadership position they were entitled to occupy.[38] Even when

Robert F. Turner, *Vietnamese Communism: Its Origins and Development* (Stanford: Hoover Institution Press, 1975), Appendices, pp. 314, 317, 324–25, 339, 349. Fall, *op. cit.*, pp. 129, 200, 230–31. Hanoi also acknowledges this fact. See "Facts about the 'Indo-China Federation' Question", in *MD*, April 11, 1978, pp. 10–17. Also, Hoang Nguyen, *op. cit.*, p. 1; *Kampuchean Dossier, I* (Hanoi: Foreign Languages Publishing House, 1978), p. 95.

35. In the 1930s, the Vietnamese failed to recruit any Kampucheans but instead concentrated on ethnic Vietnamese living in Kampuchea. After 1945, the Vietnamese did recruit some Kampucheans but did not allow them to operate as a truly autonomous communist party. Stephen P. Heder, "The Kampuchean-Vietnamese Conflict", in David W.P. Elliott (ed.), *The Third Indochina Conflict* (Boulder, Colo.: Westview Press, 1981), p. 40.

36. Huynh Kim Khanh, *Vietnamese Communism: 1925–1945* (Ithaca: Cornell University Press, 1982), p. 128.

37. Huyen, *op. cit.*, p. 220. Turner, *op. cit.*, pp. 78–79.

38. Gareth Porter, "Vietnamese Policy and the Indochina Crisis", in Elliott, *op. cit.*, pp. 87–88. It is perhaps significant to note that during her difficult negotiations with France in 1946,

the Indochinese Communist Party was dissolved into three national parties in March 1951 for strategical reasons, the concept and goal of a united Indochina remained unchanged and was explicitly incorporated into the programme of the newly formed Vietnam Workers' Party.[39] In fact, the two communist parties in Kampuchea and Laos continued to be led and controlled completely by Vietnamese cadres and their activities directed from Hanoi.[40] After all, it was the Viet Minh, i.e., the Vietnamese communists, who occupied the entire eastern part of Laos and established large pockets of guerrilla bases in Kampuchea in the early 1950s.

It would appear from the above that China's nominal interest in Kampuchea was in complete harmony with Vietnam's intensive involvement in Kampuchean affairs, thereby leaving lit-

---

Vietnam agreed completely with the French on the creation of an Indochinese Federation, except that Vietnam insisted on minimizing the French role in such a federation and at the same time magnifying her own role vis-à-vis that of either Laos or Kampuchea. Hammer, *op. cit.*, pp. 162–71.

39. As spelled out in the programme of the Vietnam Workers' Party: "The Vietnamese people must unite closely with the peoples of Laos and Kampuchea, and render them all-out support in the common struggle against imperialism, in order to liberate Indochina . . . . On the basis of the common interests of the three peoples, the Vietnamese are prepared to have long-term cooperation with Lao and Kampuchean peoples and to strive for the realization of true unity of the three peoples." Reproduced in *Xinhua yuebao* (New China Monthly) (Beijing), April 1951, pp. 1286–89. See also, *VNA*, March 21, 1951; Turner, *op. cit.*, p. 349; Fall, *op. cit.*, pp. 200, 225, 237, 276.

40. Ho Chi Minh said immediately after the dissolution of the ICP: "The creation of a separate party for each of the three states does not prejudice the revolutionary movement in Indochina . . . . The Vietnamese Party reserves the right to supervise the activities of its brother parties in Cambodia and Laos". Huyen, *op. cit.*, p. 221. Also, Michael Leifer, *Cambodia* (New York: Praeger, 1967), p. 17; Heder, *op. cit.*, p. 40.

tle ground for conflict. Unfortunately, this is not the case. As a matter of fact, China's historical recognition of Kampuchea as a separate, independent entity and her relative detachment from the latter by no means imply her complete indifference in the past to the developments in a country which lies only slightly beyond China's doorstep, much less her continuing ignorance of the strategical role Kampuchea could play in the balancing game of contemporary Southeast Asian politics. Whereas China's traditional policy of securing peace and stability along her southern borders already entailed a concern for maintaining some kind of equilibrium among her weaker neighbours, the imperial court from time to time did not hesitate to use armed forces either to restrain other southern, unruly nations which had posed a threat to China's border security, or to help put down internal rebellions in these countries upon their request.[41]

In fact, China's historical aloofness from Kampuchea must be viewed together with her age-old interest in forestalling the presence of a hostile force at least in Kampuchea's immediate eastern neighbour — Vietnam, and consequently her traditionally strong propensities to intervene in Vietnamese affairs.[42] This is not only due to the fact that strategically Vietnam constitutes the gateway to China from Southeast Asia, but also as a result of close ethnic, cultural and political links developed between the two countries over two millennia.[43] The extent to which China had gone to assist Vietnam to resist first French expansion and then French rule in Indochina merely provided the modern illustration of this well-established policy. Although Chinese political domination of Vietnam was ended 1,000 years ago, the intimate relationship forged between the

---

41. Hall, *op. cit.*, p. 176ff.
42. John King Fairbank, "A Preliminary Framework", in Fairbank, *op. cit.*, pp. 1–14; Buttinger, *op. cit.*, pp. 19–49.
43. Shao Xunzheng, *op. cit.*, p. 24ff; Hall, *op. cit.*, pp. 195–204; 644–49.

two nations during the entire anti-colonial struggle of Vietnam in the first half of the twentieth century clearly confirmed the strategical importance of Indochina to China and also somewhat revived China's traditional claim to a specially honorific status in Vietnam. Although such sentiments by no means imply an intention on the part of Beijing to re-establish the old suzerainty relationship with Vietnam, China apparently sees herself eminently qualified to remain as Vietnam's chief counsel and trusted ally. The development of any trend away from the Chinese expectations or the emergence of a hostile force in Indochina can therefore be easily perceived by Beijing as a threat to itself and could well compel China to resort to either some strategical manoeuvres or balancing acts, if only to maximize her security.[44]

If historically China has felt especially akin to Vietnam and also shown greater inclination to intervene in Vietnamese affairs, such an orientation has unfortunately not been matched by Vietnam's receptivity to Chinese influence. Although Vietnam in the past has repeatedly turned to China for help whenever in trouble, she also has a long tradition of struggle against China for political independence.[45] And precisely because of the deep-rooted cultural links with China, Vietnam after recovering her sovereignty in the tenth century has not only been determined to resist overt Chinese pressure but has also shown particular sensitivity to any sign of growth of

---

44. Shao Xunzheng, *op. cit.*, pp. 24–88; Truong Buu Lam, "Intervention Versus Tribute in Sino-Vietnamese Relations, 1788–1790", in Fairbank, *op. cit.*, pp. 165–79.

45. As one historian notes: "The Vietnamese emerged from ten centuries of Chinese occupation equipped with a warlike tradition and with probably the most keenly developed patriotism in Southeast Asia. . . . The most enduring theme in Vietnamese history is that of the struggle to preserve independence from China". Lea E. Williams, *Southeast Asia: A History* (New York: Oxford University Press, 1976), pp. 42–43. Also, Buttinger, *op. cit.*, pp. 19–49.

Chinese influence in Vietnam.[46] This age-old distrust and defiance of China, moreover, is coupled with a strong sense of pride in being, for centuries, culturally the most sophisticated nation in Southeast Asia.[47] Consequently, the attitudes Vietnam herself has held towards her weaker western neighbours are not entirely dissimilar to those which China has harboured towards Vietnam. Although Hanoi's traditional perception of Kampuchea and its intensive entanglement with Kampuchean affairs in the last three centuries or so does not necessarily imply an ambition to dominate the nation completely, both geographical proximity and recent political experience have apparently convinced Vietnam that a Kampuchea closely allied with, if not also subservient to Vietnam, constitutes one of the essential conditions of regional order and Vietnam's own security. And a Vietnam united with her two western, weaker neighbouring states would certainly greatly buttress her strength against any hostile force — be it regional or external in origin. Under any circumstances, Vietnam considers herself as having a bigger say in all matters related to Kampuchea and Laos, than any other country, let alone China which in Vietnam's view does not belong to the region and whose influence in Indochina Vietnam has been particularly wary of. And with a long tradition of intervention in Kampuchean affairs, Vietnam is also prepared to intervene again whenever necessary, if only for security considerations.

However, if China's special interest in Vietnam has met with only constant Vietnamese vigilance and misgivings, Vietnam's almost continuous territorial expansion at Kampuchea's expense and her cultural inroads in that nation have certainly been deeply resented by the Kampucheans.[48] In fact, cherishing great

---

46. See Pao-min Chang, *Beijing, Hanoi, and the Overseas Chinese* (Berkeley: Institute of Asian Studies, 1982), pp. 1–10.
47. Williams, *op. cit.*, pp. 176–77.
48. Cady, *op. cit.*, p. 114. Also, Milton E. Osborne, *Before Kampuchea* (Sydney: George Allen and Unwin, 1979), pp.

pride in being the oldest kingdom in Southeast Asia with a glorious past, Kampuchea has never been reconciled to playing a role of a passive pawn in the power politics of mainland Southeast Asia. Nor has the geographical distance that separates Kampuchea from China prevented the former from recognizing the preponderant weight China carries in regional affairs and her political value as a potential source of support to Kampuchea.[49] In fact, as militarily the weakest nation in mainland Southeast Asia, Kampuchea for centuries has developed a tradition of playing off her stronger and also more aggressive immediate neighbours, i.e., Siam and Vietnam, against each other in order to ensure her own survival. When this tactic proved somewhat ineffective within the confines of the region, the Khmer kingdom did not hesitate to look to the more distant Chinese empire, which had never posed a threat to its security, for whatever assistance might be available. Indeed, on the basis of limited records, most of the tributary missions dispatched by Kampuchea to China in the imperial period had been sent either to seek Chinese confirmation of her co-equal status with her neighbours or to request Chinese warning against their encroachments upon her independent existence.[50] Although the Chinese imperial court never had the will or capability to provide effective help to Kampuchea, it did from time to time reprimand and warn other nations in the region for their "incorrect" conduct towards Kampuchea.[51]

Moreover, if for Vietnam the French rule only buttressed her claims of special rights in Kampuchea, for Kampuchea, it clearly had the effect of keeping the Vietnamese at bay and preserving her separate identity.[52] Indeed, throughout the first

165–66; David J. Steinberg (ed.), *Cambodia: Its People, Its Society, Its Culture* (New Haven: HRAF Press, 1959), p. 41.

49. Hall, *op. cit.*, pp. 96, 127–32, 176.
50. Wang Gungwu, *op. cit.*, p. 58; Hall, *op. cit.*, pp. 96, 127–32.
51. Hall, *op. cit.*, pp. 129–31.
52. Roger E. Smith, *Cambodia's Foreign Policy* (Ithaca: Cornell University Press, 1965), p. 22.

Indochina War, Kampuchea fought single-mindedly and strenuously, at least on the diplomatic front, to regain complete control over her own destiny.[53] Nevertheless, the attainment of autonomy for Kampuchea in 1949 and final independence in 1953 did not basically alter her status and power in Indochina nor reduce her traditional reliance upon another country for survival. To the extent that Kampuchea during recent centuries suffered mainly from Vietnamese territorial annexation and cultural inroads and also considered the Vietnamese as their sworn enemy,[54] whereas historically China was more inclined to intervene in Vietnamese affairs than in the affairs of other Southeast Asian nations, the political basis for a Sino-Kampuchean alliance against an aggressive or hostile Vietnam has already been laid in the past. Indeed, the seeds of conflict between China and Vietnam over Kampuchea are in a large measure inherent in the somewhat conflicting security needs of the three nations and their unfortunately non-reciprocal images of each other. While a drastic change in the prevailing balance of power in the region in general can easily revive old aspirations, suspicions or fears between the two bigger nations and their respective weaker neighbours, a sudden deterioration of relations between Kampuchea and Vietnam, in particular, could well generate a chain reaction that will push China and Vietnam into direct confrontation.

The differences in perceptions of Kampuchea between China and Vietnam surfaced for the first time during the Geneva Conference in 1954. The organic links existing between the Vietnam Workers' Party and the two smaller communist parties in Laos and Kampuchea were so clear to everyone that Hanoi was made the spokesman for them at the conference. In fact, Pham Van Dong, the Viet Minh delegate, refused to consider the situation in Laos and Kampuchea as different from that in Vietnam, insisting that the Khmer Resistance Government and

---

53. *Ibid.,* pp. 24–86.
54. Osborne, *Before Kampuchea,* pp. 163–74.

the Pathet Lao, both created and controlled by the Viet Minh, be recognized and represented at the conference table, rather than the two royal governments still in operation.[55] Having established large pockets of operational bases in Kampuchea, the Viet Minh also refused to withdraw its forces from the two countries. As a result of the adamant attitude of Hanoi, the conference was almost stillborn.[56] It was only under the combined pressure exerted by China and the Soviet Union, and particularly to the credit of Zhou Enlai's personal diplomacy, that Hanoi was finally persuaded to accept the continuing separate existence of Kampuchea and Laos, and more importantly, the complete disbanding of the communist resistance forces in Kampuchea.[57] As a result, Kampuchea was the only country in Indochina which emerged from Geneva politically undivided. The royal government won full control over the entire area of the former French protectorate and the Viet Minh had to withdraw all its forces from the Kampuchean territory.

During the conference, China in fact expressed her eagerness to see Kampuchea and Laos becoming "independent, sovereign, and neutral", and promised to recognize the two royal governments if only they kept U.S. military bases out of their territories.[58] Although Vietnam today claims that China's policy at Geneva was aimed at dividing Indochina in order to facilitate her own domination and conquest, Beijing in the wake of the Korean War and still confronted with intense American containment was clearly preoccupied with reducing U.S. influence in Indochina rather than deliberately pitting Kampuchea against Vietnam. Nevertheless, the very fact that China was willing to sponsor a settlement that provided no communist gains at all

---

55. Leifer, *op. cit.*, p. 53; Chen, *op. cit.*, p. 310.
56. Chen, *op. cit.*, pp. 310–11; Leifer, *op. cit.*, p. 94.
57. Sir Anthony Eden, *Full Circle* (Boston: Houghton-Mifflin, 1960), p. 145.
58. Michael Field, *The Prevailing Wind* (London: Methuen, 1965), pp. 201–5. Also, Chen, *op. cit.*, p. 312.

in Kampuchea may well suggest her satisfaction with a neutral but not necessarily communist Kampuchea.[59] On the other hand, as the final agreement entailed more concessions from Vietnam than she had expected, it could not but be viewed with serious reservations by Hanoi.[60]

In fact, as soon as the Geneva Conference ended, China began to accord Kampuchea as well as Laos all the privileges and honours due a full-fledged independent state. At the Bandung Conference of 1955, Zhou Enlai assured Sihanouk that China would adhere faithfully to the five principles of peaceful co-existence with Kampuchea and reiterated China's accceptance of an independent but truly non-aligned Kampuchea.[61] In February 1956 Sihanouk visited Beijing for the first time and was treated with excessive reverence and showered with unusual hospitality.[62] As a result of the signing in June 1956 of a Sino-Kampuchean Declaration of Friendship, an economic assistance pact, and a trade agreement, Phnom Penh also became the beneficiary of the first grant-in-aid extended by Beijing to a non-communist country.[63] The rapprochement between the two countries culminated in the establishment of diplomatic relations in July 1958 when Kampuchea became the first Southeast Asian country other than North Vietnam to recognize China. This was followed immediately by a state visit of Zhou Enlai in August, and in a joint statement issued with Sihanouk in Phnom Penh, Zhou affirmed once again China's support for Kampuchea's independence, sovereignty, and territorial integrity, as well as her policy of neutrality and peace.[64]

---

59. C. P. Fitzgerald, *China and Southeast Asia Since 1945* (Hong Kong: Longman, 1973), pp. 27–28.
60. *The Truth About the Vietnam-China Relations over the Last 30 Years* (Hanoi: Ministry of Foreign Affairs, 1979), p. 12.
61. Leifer, *op. cit.*, pp. 63, 104.
62. *Renmin Ribao* (People's Daily), February 13, 1956, p. 1; Smith, *op. cit.*, p. 95.
63. *XHNA*, June 22, 1956; Leifer, *op. cit.*, p. 74.
64. G. V. Ambekar and V. D. Divekar (ed.), *Documents on China's*

Although China's posture was clearly aimed at forestalling a pro-U.S. Kampuchea and also coincided perfectly with Phnom Penh's desire to deflate the awesome pressure created by a United States closely allied with both of Kampuchea's distrusted neighbours,[65] the contrast it showed to Vietnam's policy was already revealing. While Hanoi was officially cut off from developments in Kampuchea after 1954, it did not cease penetrating the Khmer communist movement, the opposition party *Pracheachon*, and the 300,000-strong ethnic Vietnamese in the country. Apparently some of the Viet Minh units had also managed to remain in Kampuchea under a variety of disguises.[66] The fact that the Khmer Rouge now date 1960 as their founding year clearly suggests that whatever communist organizations were operating in Kampuchea in the 1950s following the Geneva Conference remained under the direction and control of Hanoi.[67] It is also noteworthy that when disputes between Phnom Penh and Saigon over the territorial issues and the Khmer minority in Vietnam heated up from 1955 on, and when border violations by South Vietnamese troops became recurrent in the late 1950s and early 1960s as a result of Saigon's attempt to pacify its western borders, Hanoi kept a strict silence on all these matters whereas Beijing almost invariably lent verbal support to Phnom Penh.[68]

Relations with South and Southeast Asia (New Delhi: Allied Publishers, Ltd., 1964), pp. 32–35.

65. Smith, *op. cit.*, pp. 91–139.
66. *Ibid.*, pp. 166, 171. Leifer, *op. cit.*, pp. 11–15; Melvin Gurtov, *China and Southeast Asia* (Baltimore: The Johns Hopkins University Press, 1975), p. 52.
67. Pol Pot claimed in 1977 that the Kampuchean Communist Party was "really born" only in 1960 when it adopted a political line independent of the Vietnamese Party. *Radio Phnom Penh*, September 28, 1977. Also see Ben Kiernan and Chanthou Boua (ed.), *Peasants and Politics in Kampuchea* (London: Zed Press, 1982), p. 293.
68. For instance, *XHNA*, August 24, 1958, May 11, 1960. Also, Leifer, *op. cit.*, pp. 96–97. Ambekar and Divekar, *op. cit.*, p. 35.

The contrast between Chinese and Vietnamese policies towards Kampuchea became even sharper in the 1960s when communist insurgency intensified in South Vietnam and as Phnom Penh deliberately drew closer to China in a bid to secure Kampuchea's territorial integrity and political independence. Starting with the conclusion of a Treaty of Friendship and Non-Aggression with Kampuchea in December 1960, Beijing not only repeatedly reassured Phnom Penh of its respect for Kampuchea as a neutral nation,[69] but also gave open and enthusiastic support to Sihanouk's proposal for an international conference to guarantee Kampuchea's neutrality and independence everytime it was made, namely in 1961, 1962, and 1963.[70] Moreover, while continuing to side with Phnom Penh in its worsening territorial dispute with Saigon,[71] Beijing in late 1963 concluded a military aid agreement with Phnom Penh and made a specific pledge to provide necessary assistance to Phnom Penh in the event of armed invasion instigated by the United States and "its vassals".[72] A similar promise was given by China in late 1964 to extend all-round support to Kampuchea if her territorial integrity and political independence were violated.[73] At about the same time, Beijing during one of Sihanouk's state visits to China even went as far as openly declaring that "an attack on

---

69. *XHNA*, December 19, 1960; May 3, 1961. Also, Harold Hinton, *Communist China in World Politics* (New York: MacMillan, 1967), p. 426; Leifer, *op. cit.*, pp. 124, 138, 174–75; *The New York Times*, October 12, 1965.

70. Leifer, *op. cit.*, pp. 103, 145; Hinton, *op. cit.*, pp. 426–27. See also, Smith, *op. cit.*, pp. 190–215. China also supported a similar proposal made by Sihanouk to guarantee Laos's neutrality in 1961, to which Hanoi was opposed. *Ibid.*, pp. 178–81.

71. Hinton, *op. cit.*, pp. 425–27.

72. Hal Kosut (ed.). *Cambodia and the Vietnam War* (New York: Facts on File Inc., 1971), p. 17; Leifer, *op. cit.*, pp. 144–45; Gurtov, *op. cit.*, p. 59.

73. Kosut, *op. cit.*, pp. 30–31; Leifer, *op. cit.*, p. 157; Gurtov, *op. cit.*, pp. 65–66.

Kampuchea is an attack on China''; the same declaration was repeated in late 1967.[74]

By all accounts, China in strengthening her ties with Kampuchea in the 1950s and 1960s was essentially responding to Sihanouk's initiatives and was also mainly concerned with securing at least a neutral rear base for growing communist activities in South Vietnam, rather than with keeping out of Kampuchea the influence of North Vietnam which after all was still negligible. Nevertheless, to the extent that Phnom Penh's increasingly pro-Beijing stance in the 1950s and the early 1960s had been generated by its age-old distrust of all Vietnamese and its growing fears first of American-South Vietnamese threat to Kampuchea's territorial integrity and then of a communist takeover of the entire Vietnam, China must have become aware of the implications of her policy.[75] In fact, the frequent trips Sihanouk made to Beijing in the 1960s, the excellent rapport he enjoyed with the Chinese leaders at least until 1967, and the outspoken personality he possessed, all suggest that the Kampuchean leader must have at least conveyed to his Chinese counterpart Kampuchea's obsessions with the Vietnamese threat, if he did not also alert China to the possible undesirable consequences a communist victory in South Vietnam might bring to the other two Indochinese states.[76] Viewed in this

---

74. *Ibid.*, pp. 65–66, 121.

75. Sihanouk throughout the 1950s and 1960s made frequent public references to the expansionist desires of Vietnam — whether communist or not. Such statements were published in Phnom Penh's major English weekly, *Realities Cambodgiennes*. See also Norodom Sihanouk, *Le Cambodge et ses Relations avec ses Voisins* (Phnom Penh: Imprimerie du Ministere de l'Information, 1962); Smith, *op. cit.*, p. 153ff, pp. 188–93; Robert Shaplen, *Time Out of Hand* (London: Andre Deutsch, 1969), pp. 312–13, 325–26.

76. In 1961, Sihanouk declared openly that he might have to ''entreat China to make North Vietnam confine itself to South Vietnam''. Quoted in Smith, *op. cit.*, p. 120. In 1966, Sihanouk

context, the degree of public support China displayed for Kampuchea throughout the 1960s could not but reveal her firm commitment to a Kampuchea free from foreign domination, be it American or otherwise. As such, it might well have been viewed in Hanoi with serious reservations.

However, in granting substantial economic, technical and military assistances to Kampuchea, China was in no position nor did she make any attempt to supplant any other major power as Phnom Penh's chief ally. China's economic aid to Kampuchea, for instance, amounted to only US$48.1 million between 1955 and 1963, which was much less than the US$85.3 million provided by the Soviet bloc or the US$309.7 million given by the United States for the same period; subsequent military aid programmes also did not match similar Soviet programmes in quantity.[77] In fact, while giving unreserved diplomatic support to the political independence and territorial integrity of Kampuchea, Beijing declined to form a military alliance with Phnom Penh as Sihanouk had requested, and somehow deliberately and repeatedly played down its commitment to the actual defence of Kampuchea, although Sihanouk consistently exaggerated it.[78] In all other respects, the Chinese government was also cautious in its approach to Kampuchea, apparently recognizing its limited capabilities and influence in a non-contiguous country. As early as November 1956, in fact, Zhou Enlai during his state visit to Kampuchea openly advised Kampuchea's Chinese minority to integrate themselves with the local people, to be model citizens, and not to engage in political activities.[79] And throughout the ensuing decade, China provided

wrote: "Peking has never ceased to display to us its comprehension and sympathy in supporting our resistance to the annexationist attempts of our neighbours". Cited in Gurtov, *op. cit.*, p. 60. See also Smith, *op. cit.*, pp. 169–72.

77. Smith, *op. cit.*, p. 123; Gurtov, *op. cit.*, p. 75.
78. Gurtov, *op. cit.*, pp. 65–66, 68–80, 136; Smith, *op. cit.*, p. 119.
79. *XHNA*, November 27, 1956; Smith, *op. cit.*, pp. 105–6; Hinton, *op. cit.*, p. 425.

neither comfort for left-wing dissidents in Kampuchea nor sanctuary for communist exiles in China.[80] With the only exception of a few months in 1967 at the height of the Cultural Revolution, when the Chinese Embassy was involved in distributing Maoist propaganda and in encouraging local Chinese to emulate the Red Guards, no attempt was made to enlist the support of the Chinese minority or local leftist groups for any political purposes.[81] And as soon as the heat of the Cultural Revolution subsided and the situation was under control in late 1967, Chinese leaders moved to reassure Sihanouk of China's peaceful intentions and reiterated their past commitments to Kampuchea.[82] The fact that Beijing decided to step up its military aid to Phnom Penh towards the end of the 1960s, in spite of Sihanouk's increasing skepticism about China's "long-term ambitions", and when North Vietnamese activities inside Kampuchea were steadily growing, further reflected China's content with an essentially neutral Kampuchea and her eagerness to preserve the status quo in that country.[83]

If Beijing's benevolence towards Kampuchea was tempered by a measure of deliberate detachment imposed by the geographical distance and China's limited capabilities, Hanoi's policy in the 1960s was characterized by an increasing ambivalence towards Kampuchea's status precisely because of Vietnam's growing involvement in an escalating war. In fact, after December 1958, when insurgency had begun in South Vietnam, Hanoi took measures to establish effective control of portions of Laotian and Kampuchean territories in order to ensure the smooth flow of materials and personnel from the

---

80. Gurtov, *op. cit.*, pp. 60–63; Leifer, *op. cit.*, p. 105.
81. Gurtov, *op. cit.*, pp. 60, 77–78; Shaplen, *op. cit.*, pp. 315, 322.
82. Shaplen, *op. cit.*, 322–24; Gurtov, *op. cit.*, p. 121. Also, Jay Taylor, *China and Southeast Asia* (New York: Praeger, 1976), pp. 145–48.
83. Gurtov, *op. cit.*, pp. 71, 75, 126, 131; Taylor, *op. cit.*, pp. 148–50.

north to the south.[84] The increasing communist activity in the south and along the Vietnamese-Kampuchean border soon led to a long series of border incidents throughout the first half of the 1960s as the Saigon forces repeatedly crossed the Kampuchean border in hot pursuit of the communists. This in turn compelled the North Vietnamese to penetrate deeper and deeper into the Kampuchean territory.[85] Apparently because of the extent of its military presence in Kampuchea and Laos, as well as the importance of the two neighbouring countries as supporting bases for communist activities in South Vietnam, Hanoi saw both Kampuchea and Laos as an integral part of its combat zone in Indochina and their securement essential to the liberation of South Vietnam. Thus, not only did Hanoi refuse to endorse Kampuchea's repeated proposal for an international conference to guarantee her independence and neutrality,[86] but also the National Front for the Liberation of South Vietnam (NFL or Viet Cong), immediately after its establishment in December 1960, announced its intention to develop "free relations with the nations of Southeast Asia, in particular with Cambodia and Laos".[87] For three consecutive years, i.e., 1960–63, the NFL in fact repeatedly demanded the formation of a confederated "peace zone" embracing Laos and Kampuchea as well as South Vietnam, to be followed subsequently by the "reunification of Vietnam through peaceful means".[88] Although the demand was mainly directed at reducing U.S. involvement in Indochina and forestalling any large-scale attack upon the communist sanctuaries in Kampuchea, the very nature

---

84. Leifer, *op. cit.*, p. 122.
85. *Ibid.*, pp. 96–99, 100, 179. Also, Kosut, *op. cit.*, pp. 13–14ff; Smith, *op. cit.*, pp. 195–210.
86. Significantly enough, both Thailand and South Vietnam rejected Sihanouk's proposal on different pretexts. Saigon also refused to sign a treaty of non-aggression with Phnom Penh. Smith, *op. cit.*, pp. 193–95, 201–2.
87. Kosut, *op. cit.*, p. 181, Hinton, *op. cit.*, p. 356.
88. Hinton, *op. cit.*, pp. 356–60.

and tone of such a proposal could not but reflect Vietnam's strategical assessment of the three Indochinese nations as interdependent and indivisible in security and defence matters, as well as her traditional paternalistic attitude towards her two weaker neighbours.[89]

Hanoi's ambivalence towards the status of Kampuchea was further shown in its persistent reluctance to recognize, openly or in writing, the territorial integrity of Kampuchea until the late 1960s, in spite of the repeated urging by Sihanouk.[90] In September 1964 Sihanouk made a special trip to Beijing to meet with North Vietnamese Premier Pham Van Dong and representatives of the NFL, in the hope of securing a formal recognition of Kampuchea's existing frontiers. But there was an apparent lack of interest in the subject on the part of both Hanoi and the Viet Cong. Pham Van Dong in fact dodged the issue by arguing that only the NFL was competent to deal with the subject and that Kampuchea should negotiate with the NFL after granting it de jure recognition.[91] When Sihanouk expressed reservations about formal recognition, Pham Van Dong simply replied that his side was prepared to wait, implying that it would be up to the communists, not Kampuchea, to suggest terms in the future.[92] In March 1965, Sihanouk at the Indochinese People's Conference of Kampucheans, North Vietnamese, and Laotians again sought support for a guarantee of Kampuchea's territorial integrity, but his efforts were firmly opposed by Hanoi.[93]

---

89. It was perhaps no accident that China's initial endorsement was quickly withdrawn when the demand was repeated. Hinton, *op. cit.*, pp. 359-60.
90. This is significant because Sihanouk's search for guarantees of Kampuchea's territorial integrity in the early 1960s was prompted by his growing fears of an imminent communist victory in South Vietnam. Shaplen, *op. cit.*, pp. 312-13, 325-26. Also, Smith, *op. cit.*, pp. 188-89; Osborne, *Before Kampuchea*, pp. 171-72.
91. Leifer, *op. cit.*, p. 157.
92. *Ibid.*, p. 158. Smith, *op. cit.*, p. 215.
93. Melvin Gurtov, "Indochina in North Vietnamese Strategy", in

In May 1966, Kampuchea adopted a different approach by proposing a treaty of friendship and non-aggression with North Vietnam and the NFL. But after eight sessions of negotiations held between Kampuchea and the NFL lasting for four months, no progress whatsoever was made, thereby once again suggesting the reluctance of the communists to offer Kampuchea assurances for the future.[94] Although the border issue between Kampuchea and Vietnam is a complex one with its roots in the colonial period, and Kampuchea certainly had been quite pompous in its overall stance and demands, the fact that North Vietnam, which did not yet share a common border with Kampuchea in those years, was unwilling to affirm at least in principle the integrity of Kampuchea's territorial sovereignty within its existing borders, probably already suggested Hanoi's essentially different perception of the entire territorial issue as well as its intention to postpone the issue until a more opportune time when Hanoi had better control of the situation.[95]

It was not until June 1967, when Sihanouk made another earnest appeal to all foreign countries to clarify their positions on the existing Kampuchean frontiers, in a renewed attempt to put a "definite and reciprocal end to all territorial claims by either Cambodia or its neighbouring countries",[96] that Hanoi and the NFL finally agreed to give written promises to respect the borders of Kampuchea.[97] But such pledges were made only

---

Joseph J. Zasloff and Allan E. Goodman (ed.), *Indochina in Conflict* (Lexington, Mass.: D. C. Heath & Co., 1972), p. 142.

94. Leifer, *op. cit.*, p. 183.

95. Sihanouk's pompous rhetoric was at least matched by Saigon's overbearing attitude towards the border issue in the late 1950s and early 1960s. Smith, *op. cit.*, pp. 156–66. For a detailed account of more recent developments, see Heder, *op. cit.*, pp. 22–34.

96. Cited in Gurtov, *China and Southeast Asia*, p. 79

97. The pledges contained loopholes that could be exploited in the future because it only recognized Kampuchea's "present frontiers" without specifying where they were. Gurtov, *op. cit.*, p. 137.

after both Moscow and Beijing had once again expressed their attitudes positively, and only in exchange for Kampuchea's full recognition of the Hanoi regime and the NFL, as well as her tacit permission to allow communist forces to operate in Kampuchea.[98] After all, by the time such pledges were made, the communists were already in control of large tracts of Kampuchean territory along the Kampuchea-Vietnam border.[99] In fact, as it turned out, the rapprochement between Kampuchea and North Vietnam, instead of resulting in more restraint on the part of North Vietnam in Kampuchea as Sihanouk had hoped, merely led to a further and rapid expansion of communist activities and areas of control. By 1969, there were already 50,000–60,000 Viet Cong and North Vietnamese troops operating in seven Kampuchean provinces bordering South Vietnam.[100] The strength and activities of the communist forces in Kampuchea had reached such levels that Sihanouk had to first make public complaints about them, then threaten to break off relations with Hanoi, and eventually order Kampuchea's weak armed forces to launch attacks upon the Vietnamese forces, in order to restrain the scope of their operation.[101] But the Vietnamese communists were already well entrenched in Kampuchea and had no intention of leaving.

---

98. *VNA*, June 12, 1967. Gurtov, *op. cit.*, pp. 79–80, 207.

99. Gurtov, *op. cit.*, p. 80.

100. Kosut, *op. cit.*, p. 53. Milton Osborne, *Region of Revolt: Focus on Southeast Asia* (London: Penguin, 1971), p. 161.

101. Kosut, *op. cit.*, p. 124; Malcolm Caldwell and Lek Tan, *Cambodia in the Southeast Asian War* (New York: Monthly Review Press, 1973), pp. 219–25. Gurtov, *op. cit.*, pp. 133–34. The Khmer Rouge reportedly also demanded in late 1969 that the NFL forces withdraw from their Kampuchean bases, and China supported the demands of both the Khmers and the Sihanouk government. *The Truth about the Vietnam-China Relations over the Last 30 Years*, p. 22. Sihanouk even secretly encouraged and supported U.S. bombing of communist sanctuaries in Kampuchea. Taylor, *op. cit.*, pp. 147–48.

2
The Precarious Triangular Alliance

Subtle but significant differences between the Chinese and Vietnamese stances on the Kampuchean situation also persisted after the rightist coup d'état of March 18, 1970. Only four days after the coup, when the new Lon Nol regime was yet to clarify its foreign policy, and even before the deposed Prince Sihanouk made public his own reaction to the incident, Hanoi was already calling resistance to Lon Nol as "part of the Indochinese people's struggle" against U.S. imperialism.[1] On March 25 Hanoi proceeded to break relations with the new Kampuchean regime and announced its full support for Prince Sihanouk and the "just struggle of the Khmer people till final victory".[2] In fact, immediately following the deposition of Sihanouk, North Vietnamese and Viet Cong forces began to expand their base areas in Kampuchea by launching a long series of attacks throughout the eastern part of the country. By the end of April, these base areas were already becoming a solid band of self-sustaining territory stretching from Laos to the sea from which any pretence of Kampuchean sovereignty was rapidly being excluded.[3] By contrast, China's attitude was more cautious. While extending the deposed prince the warmest possible

---

1. Melvin Gurtov, *China and Southeast Asia: The Politics of Survival* (Baltimore, Maryland: The Johns Hopkins University Press, 1975), p. 140.
2. *Ibid.*, pp. 140–43.
3. Hal Kosut (ed.), *Cambodia and the Vietnam War* (New York: Facts on File, Inc., 1971), pp. 125–26.

welcome and reassuring him of China's continuing recognition of him as a head of state, Beijing did not announce its position immediately nor lend any support to Vietnam's strategy of escalating the armed struggle in Kampuchea.[4] Rather, the Chinese press merely reported that the Kampuchean situation was "still developing" and that "people are closely watching the development and changes of the Kampuchean situation".[5] However, Beijing did provide Sihanouk with all the facilities necessary for coping with the crisis immediately upon his arrival in Beijing, including the broadcasting of his March 23 proclamation stating his intention to form a government in exile and to carry on an armed struggle.[6] Only on April 5 did China openly proclaim her firm support for Sihanouk when Zhou Enlai explicitly endorsed Sihanouk's policy of "defence of state sovereignty and territorial integrity".[7] But it was not until May 5, when the exiled Kampuchean government was formed, that China broke off relations with the Lon Nol regime in Phnom Penh.

With the benefit of hindsight, such discrepancies in responses may well have reflected a basic difference between China's and Vietnam's preoccupations in Kampuchea. Hanoi may well have been less averse than Beijing to the replacement of a professedly neutral but actually pro-China Kampuchean ruler whose anti-Vietnamese views had only been too well known, with a rightist but anti-China government which could now be freely and openly attacked. With more than 50,000 troops in Kampuchea and already in control of large tracts of Kampuchean territory, Hanoi probably calculated that a Vietnam-led, anti-Lon Nol

---

4. Norodom Sihanouk, *My War with the CIA* (New York: Pantheon Books, 1972), pp. 27–34.
5. *XHNA*, March 20 and 23, 1970.
6. Sihanouk, *op. cit*, p. 31.
7. *XHNA*, April 5 and 6, 1970. For the Vietnamese position, see *MD*, April 7, 1970, p. 18; April 12–13, 1970, p. 17; April 15, 1970, pp. 10–11.

military campaign could be carried out with or without Sihanouk's lending his name to it. And in view of the rudimentary character of the Khmer Rouge forces, a quick victory in Kampuchea apparently could only benefit Hanoi, as it would secure at least for Hanoi a vitally important rear base for armed actions in South Vietnam, if not also ensure its dominant position in a post-war Indochina.[8] At any rate, Hanoi now clearly counted Kampuchea as an integral part of its war effort against the United States and was therefore determined to secure and expand its sanctuaries in that country. On the other hand, China's hesitancy to commit herself openly to Sihanouk most probably reflected her uncertainty, firstly about the viability and policy posture of the new Lon Nol government,[9] and then about the feasibility of a Sihanouk-led resistance movement with communist and particularly North Vietnamese participation,[10] rather than her own reluctance to acquiesce in the already dominant position of Vietnam in Kampuchea, which

---

8. It was also a time when Hanoi advocated "big campaigns of annihilation" against the Americans and South Vietnamese troops. Jay Taylor, *China and Southeast Asia* (New York: Praeger, 1976), p. 172.

9. Sihanouk was provided with broadcasting facilities immediately after his arrival in Beijing, and started to make broadcasts to Kampuchea on March 20. Towards the end of March, there were a series of peasant uprisings in eastern Kampuchea in support of Prince Sihanouk. As a result, South Vietnamese troops were invited into Kampuchea to restore order. Sihanouk, *op. cit.*, pp. 61–62; Taylor, *op. cit.*, pp. 152–53. For a detailed analysis, see Ben Kiernan and Chanthou Boua, *Peasants and Politics in Kampuchea, 1942–1981* (London: Zed Press, 1982), pp. 206–24.

10. Sihanouk was at first undecided about his plans for the future, as he was confronted with the unpleasant dilemma between cooperating with the North Vietnamese for an uncertain future and dropping completely out of the political scene. Taylor, *op. cit.*, p. 153. Also, Norodom Sihanouk, *War and Hope* (New York: Pantheon Books, 1980), p. 123.

Beijing had always supported.[11] In fact, in view of the intense distrust held by all Khmers towards the Vietnamese and particularly the harsh criticisms made and hostile actions taken by Sihanouk against the North Vietnamese in Kampuchea during 1969–70, the Chinese might very well have been clearly advised by Sihanouk and possibly also by the Khmer Rouge this time, in the initial round of delicate negotiations between the three parties in Beijing, not to lend open encouragement to Hanoi's military posture in Kampuchea nor to merge the Khmer resistance movement with the Vietnamese activities until Hanoi's assurances of assistance without domination could be secured.[12] Whatever might have actually transpired in the months of March and April in Beijing, China apparently considered an independent Khmer resistance movement in accord with both China's model of revolutionary struggle and her well established policy of preserving the separate identity of Kampuchea. Even if Beijing did contemplate any sort of political trade with Lon Nol, as charged later by Hanoi but flatly denied by Sihanouk, it also could only indicate China's wishes to see the continuing existence of Kampuchea as a separate political entity.[13]

Viewed in this light, it is perhaps no accident that in late April of 1970, merely one month after the March coup, China, *at the request of* Sihanouk, sponsored a much publicized summit conference of the three Indochinese peoples in Guangzhou, and the conference was attended by top leaders from Vietnam, Laos,

---

11. Taylor, *op. cit.*, p. 147.
12. The Khmer Rouge's profound distrust of the North Vietnamese throughout the 1970–75 period was noted in Sihanouk, *War and Hope*, pp. 39, 47, 62–63. Also, Kiernan and Boua, *op. cit.*, p. 265; Taylor, *op. cit.*, p. 152.
13. *The Truth about Vietnam-China Relations over the Last 30 Years* (Hanoi: Ministry of Foreign Affairs, 1979), p. 29. Sihanouk, *My War with the CIA*, pp. 29, 142–43. Gurtov, *op. cit.*, p. 141. Taylor, *op. cit.*, pp. 151–52, 154.

the NFL, and Kampuchea, but with Sihanouk presiding over the meeting.[14] That such a conference was initiated by Sihanouk was significant enough, for it apparently showed the common concern of the exiled Kampucheans — both communist and non-communist — about developing an essentially nationalist movement. But the fact that it was held at all also underscored China's support for the status of Royal Kampuchea as an equal partner in a broad united front against the United States, thereby indirectly obligating the Vietnamese to grant aid without, however, becoming overbearing towards Kampuchea. The fact that the conference was chaired by a deposed Kampuchean leader who was no more than a junior partner in the proposed three-way alliance further signified clearly the importance China attached, perhaps deliberately, to the role of Kampuchea as an independent entity in the region, if not also attesting to Beijing's recognition of Phnom Penh's suspicions of Hanoi's long-term ambitions. This move could not but have irritated the Vietnamese leaders a great deal at the time.[15] Moreover, during the conference, Sihanouk with the help of the Chinese apparently succeeded in obtaining Hanoi's pledge to assist and cooperate with him on an equal footing, for the resulting agreement of the conference specifically spelled out that each of the three parties would maintain its independent identity while cooperating with the others and that the armed forces of each side should operate only within their own territories unless requested by the others.[16] In fact, throughout April and May, China was reportedly advising the North Vietnamese to build up an indigenous Khmer resistance force around the Khmer Rouge for a long-term struggle, rather than

---

14. Sihanouk, *My War with the CIA*, p. 31.
15. Hanoi later on accused China of attempting to dominate Indochina through the 1970 summit conference. *RH*, September 20, 1978. Also, *The Truth about Vietnam-China Relations over the Last 30 Years*, p. 30.
16. Sihanouk, *My War with the CIA*, pp. 172, 184, 232.

to rely overwhelmingly on Vietnamese forces and attempt a rapid conquest, which further suggested China's preference for an independent Kampuchea to one controlled by Vietnam.[17] The alliance of the three Indochinese states in general and between China and Kampuchea in particular was formalized when China took the lead in recognizing the government of the National United Front for the Liberation of Cambodia led by Sihanouk immediately after it was formed on May 5.[18] This was followed in August by the signing of a military and economic agreement between China and Sihanouk's government, and by December China had reportedly already shipped arms and equipment enough for 3,000 men into Kampuchea.[19]

However, the resulting shotgun marriage between the North Vietnamese and the Khmer resistance movement turned out to be a precarious one. In fact, for Hanoi, the summit conference of the Indochinese peoples merely provided the "legal basis" for "all-round cooperation" between Vietnam and Kampuchea, and it proceeded to expand further its areas of control in the country and even to "liberate whole provinces of Kampuchea" with its regular army.[20] Although Hanoi had agreed to train and arm an indigenous Khmer resistance force capable of independent operation in Kampuchea, in the process of doing so, it clearly attempted to regain influence over the entire Khmer communist movement.[21] In early 1970, Hanoi reportedly proposed "mixed military commands" and integration of Vietnamese cadres into the administrative organs of the exiled

---

17. *The New York Times*, May 24, 1970, p. 4. Also Gurtov, *op. cit.*, pp. 143–44.
18. *XHNA*, May 6, 1970. Hanoi followed suit on May 6. *MD,* May 8, 1970, p. 11.
19. Taylor, *op. cit.*, p. 158.
20. Hoang Nguyen, *The Vietnam-Kampuchea Conflict* (Hanoi: Foreign Languages Publishing House, 1979), pp. 8–10. See also *MD,* April 7, 1970, p. 18; April 12–13, 1970, p. 17.
21. Kiernan and Boua, *op. cit.*, pp. 257–64.

Kampuchean government.[22] Although such proposals were rejected by the Khmers, Hanoi proceeded to dispatch "a couple of thousand" Vietnamese military cadres to Kampuchea, and in the following year or so, hundreds of Kampuchean communists who had withdrawn from the country in 1954 were also sent back to Kampuchea.[23] Since these Hanoi-trained and Vietnam-based Kampuchean cadres represented a potential threat to the Paris-trained, indigenous-based Khmer leadership, the three years' cooperation between Kampuchea and Vietnam was actually marred by considerable tension generated by a latent power struggle.[24] It was apparently due to the thinly veiled enmity between the Khmers and the Vietnamese, as well as the massive Vietnamese military presence in Kampuchea, that at least from 1970 to 1972, Hanoi considered seriously the idea of using the superior Vietnamese forces on Kampuchean soil to seize control over the entire country.[25] Although Vietnam later claimed that she did not proceed with such a plan due to division in her top leadership, but rather decided to disengage herself from the Kampuchean scene in order to concentrate on the task of liberating South Vietnam, Hanoi's overbearing attitude towards Kampuchea, as well as the

---

22. Gareth Porter, "Vietnamese Policy and the Indochina Crisis," in David W.P. Elliott (ed.), *The Third Indochina Conflict* (Boulder: Westview Press, Inc., 1981), p. 91; *Livre Noire: Faits et Preuves des Actes d'Aggression et d'Annexion du Vietnam Contre le Kampuchea* (Phnom Penh, September 1978), pp. 61, 64–67, 71–72.

23. Sihanouk, *My War with the CIA*, pp. 172–74; *FEER*, April 14, 1978, p. 33.

24. *FEER*, April 14, 1978, p. 33; Hanoi claimed that skirmishes developed between the Vietnamese troops and the Khmer Rouge units as early as 1970. Nguyen, *op. cit.*, p. 10.

25. See the interview of Hoang Tung, Editor of the Vietnamese Party organ, *Nhan Dan*, with French journalists on September 7, 1978; reported by *Agence France Presse*, Hanoi, September 8, 1978.

strategical importance it attached to the country in the protracted war, was unmistakable.[26] However, as Kampuchean
forces had grown to become a credible combat force by 1972–73
and taken over the brunt of fighting against Lon No1, they
also stopped taking political guidance from Hanoi.

Vietnamese and Chinese policies towards Kampuchea
continued to diverge following the Paris Ceasefire Agreement
of January 1973, which virtually ended the cooperation between
Kampuchea and Vietnam. Immediately after the Agreement was
signed, Hanoi in a 180-degree change of policy urged Sihanouk
to negotiate with the Americans and the Lon No1 regime for
a similar peace agreement, in spite of the fact that the Khmer
Rouge already controlled ninety per cent of Kampuchea.[27] It
also cut off all aids to the Khmer Rouge, thus shifting the
burden to China completely.[28] In contrast, Beijing now pressed
for a military solution to the Kampuchean conflict and backed
up the Khmer Rouge's policy of no negotiation, no compromise,
and no coalition government.[29] So the positions of Vietnam

---

26. *Ibid.* In June 1970, at a secret meeting between North Vietnam
    and the United States, Hanoi in fact proposed a nine-point plan
    for the settlement of the war which covered all of Indochina.
    Since this was done without the knowledge of China or Sihanouk,
    Hanoi apparently was prepared to negotiate over the heads of
    its Laotian and Kampuchean allies. Taylor, *op. cit.*, p. 173.
    Former U.S. Secretary of State Dr. Kissinger also disclosed that
    in another secret meeting between the United States and North
    Vietnam in April 1970, Hanoi's negotiator Le Duc Tho empha-
    sized to him that it was Vietnam's "destiny not merely to take
    over South Vietnam, but also to dominate the whole of Indo-
    china". *The New York Times*, October 1, 1979, p. 1.
27. Gurtov, *op. cit.*, p. 188. Also, *FEER*, April 14, 1978, p. 33; April
    21, 1978, p. 16.
28. Sheldon W. Simon, "New Conflict in Indochina," *Problems of
    Communism*, September-October 1978, p. 22.
29. Gurtov, *op. cit.*, pp. 188–89. Immediately after the Paris Peace
    Agreement was signed, China endorsed the declaration made by

and China taken in 1970 were now reversed. Again with the benefit of hindsight, Vietnam may well have become wary of the increasingly independent orientation of the Khmer Rouge precisely because of the military successes the latter had been able to accumulate. A final and complete communist victory in Kampuchea that preceded a complete communist victory in South Vietnam would certainly diminish Hanoi's chances of regaining control over events in Kampuchea.[30] China, on the other hand, sided with the Khmer Rouge and favoured a final drive towards military victory for the obvious reason that the indigenous Khmers, rather than the North Vietnamese, were now in effective control, and an early victory independent of Hanoi's will or consent clearly would further bolster the image and strength of an independent Kampuchea. Although the Chinese position need not have been directed against Vietnam any more than the Vietnamese position was directed against China, both nations could not but have become increasingly concerned about the possible implications of the rapidly changing balance of power in Indochina at the time.

Indeed, if China's support for Kampuchea so far had been mainly deterrent and passive in nature, i.e., to restrain the massive power of a hostile United States by maintaining a neutral friend in Indochina, the 1973 Ceasefire Agreement was a turning point in Sino-Kampuchean and Sino-Vietnamese rela-

---

Sihanouk and Khieu Samphan in early February which reiterated their determination to overthrow the Lon Nol regime by force. *BR*, February 11, 1973, p. 8. On April 12, 1973, Zhou Enlai at a banquet in honour of Sihanouk returning from a much publicized trip to the liberated areas in Kampuchea, pledged that the Chinese people would continue to support the Kampuchean people until final victory. *Renmin Ribao* (People's Daily), April 13, 1973, p. 2.

30. The Vietnamese traditionally viewed Kampuchea and Laos as secondary areas of revolutionary struggle which served the needs of the Vietnamese revolution and which would be liberated only after Vietnam was liberated. See Porter, *op. cit.*, pp. 86–87.

tions as a result of the rapid American withdrawal from the entire mainland Southeast Asia and the growing influence of the Soviet Union in North Vietnam, which immensely improved the prospect of attaining final victory for the communists. Since the Khmer resistance movement under the nominal leadership of Sihanouk was much weaker than the North Vietnamese and also represented a force which the Soviet Union had never supported, and in view of the age-old resentment held by the Khmers towards the Vietnamese and their new fears, Beijing apparently felt that to buttress further the status and strength of the Khmers should be in the long-term interest of both Kampuchea and regional stability. It would also ensure a more desirable balance of forces in China's southern flank and present a counter-weight to Soviet influence in the region, if not also restraining the possible ambitions of Vietnam. The exiled Kampucheans certainly were eager to keep China on their side if only to ensure total control of their own destiny at a crucial time in their revolutionary struggle.[31] Whatever role the Khmer Rouge and Sihanouk themselves might have played in the crystallization of such a policy, the security needs of Kampuchea now apparently coincided perfectly with those of China, and Beijing certainly began to take more initiative in shaping the developments in Indochina.

China's determination to play up the role of Kampuchea vis-à-vis Vietnam was amply shown in her growing economic and military aid to the country. Just before the conclusion of the Paris Agreement, China signed two agreements with the

---

31. The Khmer Rouge themselves disclosed that in 1973, they "told the Chinese comrades that the Kampuchean revolution is independent and sovereign but if the Kampuchean revolution had bound itself with Vietnam, it would not be able to wage the struggle, because even in the bosom of the Party, there would not be unanimity". Ben Kiernan, "Conflict in the Kampuchean Communist Movement", *Journal of Contemporary Asia*, Vol. 10, Nos. 1-2 (1980), p. 10.

royal government in exile on the gratuitous supply of military equipment and economic assistance.[32] In fact, immediately after the Peace Agreement was signed, Beijing reportedly asked the Vietnamese to transfer their military equipments and arms in the south to the Khmers in order to help the latter liberate their country.[33] On May 27, 1974, another agreement was concluded between Beijing and the Khmers to ensure continuing flow of military supplies from China to Kampuchea.[34] These postures appeared all the more significant against the background of a progressive reduction of Chinese aid to Vietnam beginning in 1973.[35] In the meantime, throughout the 1973–75 period, Beijing made sure that Kampuchean leaders never for a moment dropped out of the limelight in China and continued to receive the best possible treatment in Beijing. This included an annual, much publicized celebration held in commemoration of the establishment of Sihanouk's government-in-exile, often accompanied by editorials and pictures of Kampuchean leaders in the newspapers.[36] In April 1974, Mao even granted an audience to all the top Kampuchean leaders in spite of his failing health.[37] But that was not all. While expressing repeatedly and consistently China's support for a military solution to the war in Kampuchea, Beijing reportedly contended as late as early 1975 that the struggle in Vietnam would take a long time to complete

---

32. *BR*, January 22, 1973, p. 5.
33. Vietnam claimed that this was a deliberate policy of creating difficulties for Vietnam's own armed struggle. *The Truth about the Vietnam-China Relations over the Last 30 Years*, p. 34.
34. *XHNA*, May 27, 1974.
35. *Vietnam Courier* (Hanoi), July 1978, pp. 4–5. Beijing also admitted that it reduced its aid to Vietnam after 1973, in order to "catch its breath back". *BR*, July 28, 1978, p. 28.
36. *Renmin Ribao*, March 23, 1971, p. 1; March 24, 1971, p. 3; March 23, 1972, pp. 1–2; March 24, 1972, p. 1; March 23, 1973, p. 1; March 24, 1973, p. 1; March 24, 1974, p. 1; March 23, 1975, p. 1; March 24, 1975, p. 1.
37. *XHNA*, April 2, 1974.

and counselled Hanoi to "take a low posture for at least a couple of years".[38] Although China's policy towards the Khmer Rouge after 1973 was clearly in accord with the wishes of the exiled Kampucheans, if not in fact actively promoted by them, the apparently preferential treatment Beijing extended to Kampuchea and the higher priority it gave to her liberation could not but have been viewed by Hanoi with much misgivings. Indeed, having always had reservations about China's enthusiasm in supporting Kampuchea, and with a diametrically opposed conception of Kampuchea's role in regional stability, the Vietnamese must have seen China's new posture as a deliberate attempt to detach Kampuchea from Vietnam and therefore to undermine Vietnam's status in Indochina.[39]

If from 1973 onwards China became more concerned about the growing Soviet influence in Southeast Asia and therefore more eager to keep Kampuchea as her ally, Vietnam was certainly also determined to retain her physical presence and political influence in Kampuchea, in order to ensure a close relationship after the war was over. Thus, one cannot discard entirely the allegations made by the Khmer Rouge that Hanoi after 1973 suddenly pressed for closer coordination with the Khmer Rouge and refused to hand over the control of certain Kampuchean territories back to them.[40] It was perhaps also no

---

38. *Vietnam Courier*, June 1979, p. 10. Also, Porter, *op. cit.*, pp. 75–76.
39. See *The Truth about the Vietnam-China Relations over the Last 30 Years*, pp. 11–31.
40. According to Sihanouk, as soon as the Paris Ceasefire Agreement was signed, the Khmer Rouge began to expel ethnic Vietnamese from Kampuchea and demanded Vietnamese troops to move out of Kampuchean territory. Instead of evacuating, however, the Vietnamese strengthened their presence and control and sought to win over segments of the Khmer Rouge to their side. See Sihanouk, *War and Hope*, pp. 22–23. Also, Wilfred Burchett, *The China-Cambodia-Vietnam Triangle* (London: Zed Press, 1981), pp. 146–52, 172–73.

accident that skirmishes and border disputes began to surface and escalate between the North Vietnamese and the Khmer Rouge in 1973. Most of the armed clashes taking place between them clearly resulted from Hanoi's efforts of at least holding on to, if not in fact also expanding, its well-established sanctuaries in Kampuchea, and the Khmer Rouge's attempt to regain control over them.[41] Moreover, in April 1975, in spite of its earlier disengagement from the military activities in Kampuchea and the pressing need for manpower in its own campaign against Saigon, Hanoi threw in at least two army divisions of its regular troops in the final battle of Phnom Penh, apparently in an attempt to gain a new foothold in Kampuchea after the communist victory.[42]

On the other hand, alarmed by the rapid rapprochement between Beijing and Washington, and with China already replaced by the Soviet Union as the principal supplier of arms and political supporter in 1973, Hanoi also came to question the continuing value of its close ties with China. Indeed, whether to win Kampuchea over to the Vietnamese side or to reassert her complete political independence from China, it was necessary for Vietnam to stand up squarely against China now. It was thus perhaps no accident that beginning in late 1973 and throughout 1974, Hanoi raised a number of issues with China over territorial matters, first concerning the land border, and

---

41. Stephen P. Heder, "The Kampuchean-Vietnamese Conflict", in Elliott, op. cit., pp. 27–28. Also, FEER, October 1, 1973, pp. 13–14.
42. See Huang Hua's revelations in a confidential talk to high-ranking cadres in July 1977. Translated in King C. Chen (ed.), China and the Three Worlds (New York: MacMillan Co., 1979), p. 269. In late 1974, the combined North Vietnamese-Viet Cong forces in South Vietnam were estimated to be around 190,000 men. By the end of March 1975, Hanoi was said to have 275,000 men in the south. Apparently most reinforcements were made by transferring troops from other parts of Indochina. The New York Times, March 31, 1975.

then on the Gulf of Tonkin and finally on the South China
Sea islands, all of which had hardly been disputed before.[43]
Particularly in early 1974, Vietnam expressed open reservations
about China's war with the Saigon regime over the Paracels.
In August of the same year, Hanoi demanded a delineation of
the Gulf of Tonkin that would give Vietnam a greater share
of its water area than it would China. In October, Hoang Tung,
Editor-in-Chief of the Vietnamese official newspaper, *Nhan
Dan*, in a public interview told foreign newsmen that China
"is not a country of this region and should not have as much
offshore waters as it has claimed", thereby openly questioning
China's claims to all the South China Sea islands.[44] If Beijing
was merely aware of Vietnam's manoeuvres in Kampuchea but
still unsure of her intentions there, the nature and timing of
Hanoi's territorial demands on China could not but have
revealed to Beijing Vietnam's ambitions. Vietnam's seizure in
April 1975 of the six Spratly islands occupied by Saigon troops,
even before the fall of Saigon, must have further confirmed
Beijing's suspicions. It certainly had the effect of making China
more sympathetic to Kampuchea in the latter's emerging border
dispute with Vietnam. Indeed, from Beijing's perspective, if
Vietnam could be so daring as to go against her long-time
benefactor, China, she must have been practising outright
hegemonism towards her own junior partner and weaker
neighbour, Kampuchea. Whichever side had actually initiated
acts seen as unfriendly by the other side, the series of small steps
taken by both China and Vietnam clearly led to a thickening
of an atmosphere of mutual distrust between the two countries
and began to generate considerable ill-feelings.

The double victory the communists achieved in Kampuchea
and Vietnam in April 1975 finally marked the watershed for

---

43. For a detailed analysis, see Pao-min Chang, "The Sino-
    Vietnamese Territorial Dispute," *Asia-Pacific Community*,
    Spring 1980, pp. 130–65.
44. *The Voice of the Nation* (Bangkok), November 23, 1974.

both Vietnamese-Kampuchean and Sino-Vietnamese relations. As long as the communist takeover in the two countries remained a goal and China played the crucial supporter of both Vietnam and Kampuchea, there were still sufficient incentives for the North Vietnamese and the Khmers to coexist and cooperate with each other amicably. It was also possible for China to avoid taking sides, at least openly. But the end of the war not only immediately reduced China's influence in both countries, but also quickly revived the age-old fears of Phnom Penh and the traditional aspirations of Hanoi, which in turn entailed a qualitative change in China's relations with the two countries respectively. From the Vietnamese point of view, the communist victory in Kampuchea would not have been a reality without Vietnamese assistance during the crucial war years; nor could Vietnam's security be ensured without a close relationship with Kampuchea.[45] Hanoi therefore asked for and also felt entitled to a special status in Kampuchea and reportedly once again demanded "common diplomatic and economic policies" and even a "united party" and a "united army" with Kampuchea.[46] Indeed, as China appeared to be wooing Kampuchea at a time when Vietnam had decided to move away from China, it was all the more necessary to solidify the wartime unity between the two countries. From the Kampuchean point of view which China shared, precisely because of the prolonged dominant role of Vietnam in Kampuchea, if not also her

---

45. In 1978, Hoang Tung, Editor of *Nhan Dan*, referring to the situation in the early 1970s, told foreign journalists: "At first, it was our troops which did the fighting, defeating the US-Saigon operations and Lon Nol's two campaigns — Chenla I and II. China gave material aid to Kampuchea, but who transported them? It was our shoulders, our means, our flesh and blood that carried all that the Chinese gave to Kampuchea." *FEER*, April 21, 1978, p. 18. Sihanouk also admitted all this. See his *War and Hope*, pp. 25–26; *FEER*, June 16, 1983, p. 13.
46. *XHNA*, June 20, 1978. For charges made by the Khmer Rouge, see for instance, *Radio Phnom Penh*, April 29, June 5, 1978.

expressly overbearing attitude towards Kampuchea, a close relationship with Hanoi could only be a prelude to eventual Vietnamese domination. Phnom Penh also insisted that Hanoi withdraw all its troops from Kampuchea as it had promised,[47] now that the war was over, for their continuing presence constituted a serious threat to Kampuchea's security and stability. Indeed, in view of the pervasive Vietnamese influence developed over the war years, no Kampuchean regime could feel secure until the problem was reduced to manageable levels.[48] The precarious triangular alliance was made all the more untenable by the emergence of a vehemently nationalistic new regime in Phnom Penh which — not entirely a surprise in itself — once set up, proceeded to purge all Vietnam-trained cadres, disband all Hanoi-initiated organizations, and expel all Vietnamese civilians in Kampuchea.[49] Skirmishes between the Khmers and the Vietnamese forces along the Vietnam-Kampuchea border, which reportedly had started as early as 1973, now quickly developed into major armed clashes.[50] In fact, intensely jealous of its newly gained independence and blinded by its rapid ascendance to power, the new Khmer regime once again echoed its predecessors' claims to territories in the Mekong Delta area long lost to Vietnam and vowed repeatedly

---

47. Pham Van Dong in March 1970 expressly promised Sihanouk that Vietnam would fully respect Kampuchea's independence, sovereignty and territorial integrity within their present borders once the war was ended. Cited by Sihanouk in his message of thanks to Pham Van Dong on March 26, 1970. *RH*, May 11, 1970.

48. Porter, *op. cit.*, p. 92.

49. Joseph J. Zasloff and MacAlister Brown, "Passion of Kampuchea", *Problems of Communism*, January-February 1979, pp. 34-37; *FEER*, January 13, 1978, pp. 13-14; April 21, 1978, pp. 20-21. Francois Ponchaud, *Cambodia Year Zero* (London: Penguin, 1977), p. 157.

50. In April 1977, there were still 20,000 Vietnamese troops in Kampuchea. *FEER*, May 9, 1979, p. 20.

to recover such territories and to restore the glory of the old Khmer empire.[51]

To what extent was the new Khmer regime's anti-Vietnamese policy deliberately designed to engulf China in its conflict with Vietnam probably will never be known to the outside world. But Hanoi apparently watched the developments in Kampuchea with grave concern. Precisely because of Phnom Penh's intense hostility towards Vietnam, Hanoi found it necessary also to adopt a deliberate hard-line position on Kampuchea, for to do otherwise would only fan further the xenophobia of the new regime. This perhaps explains why, although negotiations on border disputes were held in June 1975 almost immediately after the communist victories in both countries and on a number of other occasions thereafter, all yielded no results due to the intransigence displayed by both sides.[52] At a meeting held in May 1976 between representatives of the two parties, Hanoi reportedly went back on their war-time commitments to respect the existing borders of Kampuchea by arguing that such pledges had been made under the pressures of war against U.S. imperialism, and that the pre–1954 French maps of Indochina delineated only the "administrative and police" jurisdiction of Cochinchina and Kampuchea, leaving aside the question of their territorial sovereignty unsettled.[53] Vietnam thus proposed a new boundary line which presumably incorporated at least some,

---

51. *Radio Phnom Penh*, May 10, 1978. As late as mid-April, Pol Pot in a broadcast interview reaffirmed Kampuchea's claim to Cochin China and demanded change of land and sea borders. *Keesing's Contemporary Archives*, October 27, 1978, p. 29273. Also, Kiernan, "Conflict in the Kampuchean Communist Movement", pp. 13–15; Sihanouk, *War and Hope*, pp. 37–38, 46, 50–51, 81.

52 See *MD*, January 12, 1978, pp. 6–7; *Vietnam Courier*, February 1978, pp. 6–7; *Radio Phnom Penh*, April 29, 1978; Heder, *op. cit.*, pp. 27–34.

53. *Vietnam Courier*, February 1978, p. 6; *Vietnam* (Hanoi), June 1978, p. 3. It is noteworthy that Hanoi advanced a similar argu-

if not all of the former Vietnamese sanctuaries into Vietnamese
territory, as well as a maritime boundary line which would give
more territorial waters to Vietnam than the French colonial
maps warranted. The Vietnamese proposal was naturally completely unacceptable to Kampuchea.[54] Convinced that
Vietnam was bent on annexing Kampuchea and also blinded
by its xenophobia and conceit, Phnom Penh from then on
simply refused to negotiate with Hanoi any more and preferred
to launch sporadic raids on Vietnamese troops in Kampuchean
territory in order to push them out.[55]

The deterioration of Kampuchean-Vietnamese relations after
1975 appeared all the more abrupt and significant against the
backdrop of a further strengthening of ties between Beijing and
Phnom Penh, as shown in the massive influx of Chinese
technicians into Kampuchea to help with her post-war
reconstruction.[56] In September 1975, when Sihanouk returned
to Kampuchea following China's advice, Beijing granted
Phnom Penh a most generous interest-free loan of US$150
million plus a non-repayable subsidy of US$20 million to cover
Kampuchea's foreign trade deficit.[57] Although China's aid to
Kampuchea represented a continuation of her well-established
policy, compared with the termination of all Chinese non-
refundable aid to Vietnam by the end of 1975, Beijing's inten-

---

ment in its territorial dispute with China over the South China
Sea islands. See Chang, *op. cit.*, pp. 144–45.
54. *Radio Phnom Penh*, April 29, 1978; *Vietnam Courier*, February
    1978, p. 4; *BR*, July 21, 1978, p. 6. Also, Heder, *op. cit.*,
    pp. 31–34.
55. Heder, *op. cit.*, pp. 27–34. *Vietnam Courier*, February 1978, pp.
    2–4; Nguyen, *op. cit.*, pp. 21–22; *MD*, January 12, 1978, pp.
    9–10; *Radio Phnom Penh*, May 10, 1978.
56. Scholars differ on the extent of Chinese presence in Kampuchea
    during 1975–1976. But presumably it was kept at a minimum by
    Kampuchea. See Ponchaud, *op. cit.*, p. 104; Sihanouk, *War and
    Hope*, pp. 135–36; Zasloff and Brown, *op. cit.*, p. 39.
57. Ponchaud, *op. cit.*, p. 103.

tion of boosting the strength of Kampuchea vis-à-vis Vietnam was once again apparent to all.[58] However, it is noteworthy that, though virtually the only ally of Kampuchea, Beijing for nearly two years after April 1975 was hardly willing or able to control the events in a country engulfed by revolutionary fanaticism. In fact, the ultra-nationalistic and isolationist orientation of the new Khmer regime reduced to a bare minimum all consultation and coordination on policy issues between the two countries as early as September 1975.[59] The series of internal crises that shook the Chinese natural and political scenes in the year of 1976 further prevented Beijing from taking more than a nominal interest in Kampuchea. Thus, in spite of the substantial Chinese presence in the country, Beijing could neither exert any moderating influence over Phnom Penh's drastic programmes of socio-economic transformation, nor prevent the massive persecution of nearly half a million ethnic Chinese in Kampuchea. Whereas the adamantly anti-Vietnamese stance Phnom Penh took certainly required no instigation from Beijing, whatever advice of caution Beijing might have given to the Khmer leaders on the border conflict had apparently all fallen upon deaf ears.[60] In fact, Phnom Penh demonstrated its jealously guarded independence by placing Sihanouk under house arrest in early 1976, apparently against China's will, and by forbidding the prince even to send messages of condolence to Beijing upon Mao's death in September 1976.[61]

---

58. *The Truth about the Vietnam-China Relations over the Last 30 Years*, pp. 32, 39; *FEER*, December 9, 1977, p. 38.
59. Zasloff and Brown, *op. cit.*, pp. 33, 39. After Khieu Samphan went to Beijing to accompany Sihanouk back to Phnom Penh in late August of 1975, no top ranking Kampuchean delegations visited China again until late 1977. *BR*, August 29, 1975, p. 7.
60. Zhou Enlai in his sick bed reportedly counselled Khieu Samphan against radicalism when the Kampuchean leader was in Beijing in August 1975. Sihanouk, *War and Hope*, p. 86; Ponchaud, *op. cit.*, p. 160. Also, *FEER*, September 8, 1978, pp. 11–12.
61. *ST*, January 23, 1979, p. 17. China had hoped that Sihanouk's

It also expressed displeasure over China's leadership change in late 1976 by refusing to congratulate Beijing on the fall of the ultra-leftist "gang of four". Nor did it send delegates to attend the new Eleventh Party Congress held in August 1977, following the political crisis.[62]

However, Beijing's continuing support for a vehemently anti-Vietnamese Kampuchea was sufficient proof to Hanoi of China's culpability in the strained relations between Hanoi and Phnom Penh. And from the Vietnamese point of view, the fanatic nature of the new Khmer regime only rendered Beijing's motivation in aligning itself with Phnom Penh all the more suspicious. As Hanoi could not tolerate — and yet Beijing appeared to be condoning — a Kampuchea openly hostile to Vietnam, what had originally been a localized Kampuchean-Vietnamese dispute was doomed to explode into a larger conflict between China and Vietnam. And now it was only natural for Hanoi to adopt a high-posture approach in handling the problems of Laos and Kampuchea and at the same time to solicit openly Moscow's backing in its possible confrontation with China. As a matter of fact, in July 1976, Hoang Tung, Editor-in-Chief of *Nhan Dan*, both confirmed and explained in the hitherto clearest terms Vietnam's continuing tilt towards the Soviet Union, when he told a Swedish newsman: "During the war, it was vital for Vietnam that both China and the USSR helped North Vietnam to the full. Today, it is no longer so vital for this country to follow that policy.... Both the political and cultural pressure from the north must be neutralized, and here the rapprochement with the USSR plays a very important role for Vietnam today. There is a tangibly strong Soviet interest coinciding with Vietnamese interests — to reduce

---

return to Kampuchea could temper the revolutionary ardour of the new regime. Ponchaud, *op. cit.*, p. 160. Also, *BR*, September 12, 1975, pp. 8–9; *FEER*, April 14, 1978, pp. 39–40.

62. *ST*, January 23, 1979, p. 17; *FEER*, March 26, 1976, p. 24; October 7, 1977, p. 87.

Chinese influence in this part of the world".[63] Moreover, the Fourth Congress of the Vietnamese Communist Party held in December 1976 not only resulted in the purge of the pro-China faction and the ascendence of the pro-Soviet faction of the Vietnamese leadership, but also adopted a resolution which stated in unequivocal terms Vietnam's long-term goal in Kampuchea. The resolution proclaimed Hanoi's policy in Indochina as "to preserve and develop the *special* relationship between the Vietnamese people and the peoples of Laos and Cambodia and to strengthen the military solidarity, mutual trust, long-term cooperation and mutual assistance in all fields . . . so that the three countries, which have been associated with one another in the struggle for national liberation, will be associated *forever* with one another in the building and defence of their respective countries".[64]

The year 1977 thus witnessed a sudden and conspicuous escalation of Vietnam's tilt towards the Soviet Union, as evident in the exchange of numerous delegations and the conclusion of countless cooperation or aid agreements in all fields between Hanoi on the one hand and Moscow and its East European allies on the other.[65] While all the Vietnamese VIPs, including Pham Van Dong, Vo Nguyen Giap, Troung Chinh, and Le Duan, had a chance to visit Moscow in the course of 1977, it is perhaps significant that the high-level exchanges began with a prolonged visit of a Vietnamese military delegation to Moscow and other Warsaw Pact capitals from March to May and culminated in the return visit of a Soviet military delegation

---

63. Reported in *Defense and Foreign Affairs Daily* (U.S.A.), July 13, 1976 and quoted in *XHNA*, April 2, 1979. See also, Porter, *op. cit.*, p. 78.
64. Communist Party of Vietnam, *Fourth National Congress: Documents* (Hanoi: Foreign Languages Publishing House, 1977), pp. 248–49. Also reiterated in *RH*, May 9, 1978.
65. This is quite evident from a cursory examination of *MD*, February-December 1977.

to Hanoi in October.[66] With Soviet reassurances of political support, Vietnam apparently gained new confidence in confronting both China and Kampuchea. Thus, in early 1977, Hanoi intensified its drive to integrate — or rather to discriminate against — the ethnic Chinese in Vietnam, to be followed soon by the launching of a "border purification" campaign along the Sino-Vietnamese border that already resulted in the expulsion of border residents into Chinese territory.[67] Both measures were taken apparently in anticipation of an impending deterioration of Sino-Vietnamese relations. In the meantime, Hanoi also became increasingly outspoken and adamant in its continuing territorial dispute with China.[68] In fact, starting with a major incident taking place at the border town of Yuyiguan (Friendship Gate) in May as a result of scuffles between the two sides, the Sino-Vietnamese land border was not to see tranquillity for a long time.[69]

Hanoi's new stance on China was further coupled with an escalation of its military and political pressures on Kampuchea, as shown in the outbreak of large-scale fighting in late April and May of 1977, and again from June to August, between the Khmer forces and some 20,000 Vietnamese troops still entrenched in their long-time enclaves in Kampuchea.[70] There were also recurrent reports of Vietnamese sabotage and coup attempts throughout 1977.[71] On July 18, Hanoi finally formal-

---

66. *MD*, March 9, August 5, September 6, and October 11, 1977. Also, *FEER*, November 11, 1977, p. 32.
67. See Pao-min Chang, "The Sino-Vietnamese Dispute over the Ethnic Chinese", *The China Quarterly*, June-August 1982, pp. 203–4.
68. Chang, "The Sino-Vietnamese Territorial Dispute", pp. 144–50.
69. *Ibid*. China reported about 400 border incidents in 1975, nearly 700 in 1976, and over 900 in 1977. The Vietnamese figures are 294 for 1975, 812 for 1976, and 973 for 1977. See *BR*, March 30, 1979, p. 19; *Vietnam Courier*, March 1979, p. 8.
70. Heder, *op. cit.*, pp. 32–34; Simon, *op. cit.*, p. 28.
71. Sihanouk, *War and Hope*, p. 75. Vietnam also reported

ized its dominant position in Laos and therefore completed the first phase of its Indochina plan when it concluded a Treaty of Friendship and Cooperation with Laos, which not only justified the presence of 50,000 Vietnamese troops on Laotian soil, but also sanctioned all-round cooperation between the two countries.[72] Once again, Hanoi made no pretentions of its aims in Indochina, as the treaty obligated the two countries to pledge to "protect and develop the *special* Vietnamese-Lao relationship in order to make the two countries, *inherently united* in the national liberation cause, remain united *forever* in national construction and defence". In an accompanying joint communique, the two parties also affirmed that they would "do everything in their power to strengthen the militant solidarity, lasting cooperation, and mutual assistance among the fraternal peoples of Vietnam, Laos, and Kampuchea.[73] The treaty was also meant to seal the bonds between Vietnam and Laos permanently as it was valid for twenty-five years, to be automatically renewed for successive periods of ten years.

Having more or less begun to recover from the political earthquake of 1976 and therefore to renew its interest in Indochina, Beijing must have watched all these developments with growing concern. In the eyes of Beijing, Hanoi's open profession and solicitation of a permanent, intimate relationship with its weaker neighbours was a concrete manifestation of Vietnam's intention to dominate the entire Indochina. The worsening of the territorial dispute and the surfacing of a new, ethnic dispute between China and Vietnam merely demonstrated to China the scope of Vietnam's ambitions in the region. Moreover, to the extent that Moscow had expressed enthusiastic support for Vietnam on all the issues of her bilateral dispute with China, Beijing could not but view Hanoi's tilt towards

---

numerous uprisings in eastern Kampuchea from late 1976 through 1977. Nguyen, *op. cit.*, pp. 29–30.
72. *RH*, July 19, 1977; *ST*, July 20, 1977, p. 1.
73 *RH*, July 18, 19, 1977.

the Soviet Union as an ominous sign of Vietnamese-Soviet collusion against China. Indeed, from China's perspective, Vietnam's new stances towards Kampuchea and China could not have been taken so blatantly without Soviet encouragement or support. As such, they presented not only a direct threat to the security of Kampuchea and a clear challenge to China's status in the region, but also pointed to a rapid expansion of Soviet influence in Indochina which must now be taken seriously. Although China continued to refrain from taking sides openly in the rapidly worsening Vietnamese-Kampuchean conflict, signs of her disagreement and displeasure with Vietnam's Kampuchea policy, as well as her disconcert with the looming shadow of Soviet presence in the region, did become increasingly clear in the course of 1977. In a number of statements made early in the year, China not only repeatedly lent verbal support to Kampuchea's "independence, sovereignty, and territorial integrity", and commended the Kampuchean people for having "persevered in the struggle against imperialism, colonialism, and hegemonism" and "succeeded in frustrating sabotage by foreign and domestic enemies", but also pointedly warned the Vietnamese of the danger of social imperialism.[74] That the signing of the Vietnam-Laos Treaty in July went almost completely unreported in Beijing also revealed China's misgivings about the treaty's implications.[75] In fact, by late July, China had already made a veiled warning to Vietnam, though still privately, that she would "not watch indifferently any intervention in Kampuchean sovereignty or coveting of Kampuchean territory by social imperialism" and would "support Kampuchea and her people in their struggle and in their actions to protect Kampuchea's territorial integrity and national sovereignty by giving *all possible* assistance".[76] The schism between China and Vietnam over Kampuchea was rapidly widening.

---

74. *BR*, January 14, 1977, pp. 7, 25; April 22, 1977, pp. 40–44.
75. It was only briefly noted in *Renmin Ribao*, July 21, 1977, p. 5.
76. See Huang Hua's talks in Chen, *op. cit.*, pp. 272–73.

3
Towards Open Conflict

If Hanoi's open proclamations of its objectives in Indochina and the increasing assertiveness of its policy towards China reflected Vietnam's growing confidence in handling the troubled relations with her two neighbouring states, Beijing's approach and reaction to Vietnam appeared to be still restrained throughout the year of 1977. Apparently reluctant to exacerbate a conflict which she had only marginal control or to commit herself unequivocably to a country whose policy had been at best unpredictable, China continued to maintain overt neutrality in the worsening Vietnam-Kampuchea conflict and confined her efforts mainly to alerting Vietnam to the danger of growing Soviet influence in Southeast Asia and encouraging Kampuchea to negotiate with Vietnam.[1] In fact, while the Chinese aid to Kampuchea before mid-1978 was limited both in scope and volume and was designed only to boost the country's defence capabilities,[2] Beijing some time in the spring of 1977 made a four-point proposal to bring about a negotiated settlement of the Vietnam-Kampuchea border dispute and even offered to mediate in the conflict.[3] In June, Chinese Vice Premier Li

---

1. Stephen P. Heder, "The Kampuchean-Vietnamese Conflict", in David W.P. Elliott (ed.), *The Third Indochina Conflict* (Boulder: Westview Press, Inc., 1981), pp. 43–47. See also Huang Hua's confidential talks given in late July of 1977 and translated in King C. Chen (ed.), *China and the Three Worlds* (New York: MacMillan Co., 1979), pp. 270–72.
2. Heder, *op. cit.*, p. 58; *FEER*, July 14, 1978, p. 7.
3. Chen *op. cit.*, pp. 271–72.

Xiannian in a memorandum presented to visiting Vietnamese
Premier Pham Van Dong reminded the Vietnamese leader of
the "intimate relationship between China and Vietnam"
developed over "long years of arduous struggle" and the fact
that the two countries were "linked by common mountains and
rivers and closely related as lips and teeth". While Li painstakingly but politely drew Dong's attention to the unfortunate
developments regarding territorial and ethnic issues, he
pointedly avoided any mention of the Kampuchean situation.[4]
Meanwhile, Beijing continued to give "cordial and friendly"
welcomes to visiting Vietnamese dignatories, and refrained from
criticizing Vietnamese actions.[5] China apparently hoped that,
with a low-keyed public posture and more private consultations,
Vietnam could probably be persuaded to dissociate herself from
the Soviet Union.[6] And as long as Hanoi kept a distance from
Moscow, the Vietnam-Kampuchea conflict should be amenable
to a solution reasonably satisfactory to all the parties concerned.

Whatever self-restraint Beijing might be still exercising in 1977
in order to avert a final split with Hanoi, however, was quickly
offset by Phnom Penh's bold military initiatives against
Vietnam and the latter's increasingly large-scale counter-
offensives against Kampuchea.[7] On the one hand, the Phnom
Penh regime, in addition to being still under the spell of its
xenophobia, probably also became wary of the possibility of
a Sino-Vietnamese compromise over Kampuchea, which
conceivably could only work in Vietnam's favour. On the other
hand, Hanoi might well have also taken China's overt neutrality
in the border conflict and her relative inaction on the other

---

4. See Li's Memorandum to Pham Van Dong released in *BR*,
   March 30, 1979, pp. 19–22; *XHNA*, July 18, 1979.
5. Robert G. Sutter, "China's Strategy toward Vietnam and the
   Implications for the United States," in Elliott, *op. cit.*, pp.
   174–75.
6. *Ibid.*, p. 174. Also, Heder, *op. cit.*, pp. 45–47.
7. Heder *op. cit.*, pp. 32–34; Gareth Porter, "Vietnamese Policy
   and the Indochina Crisis," in Elliott, *op. cit.*, pp. 96–98.

issues of bilateral dispute as a sign of China's acquiescence in Hanoi's new posture towards Kampuchea, if not in fact her inability to intervene.[8] Whatever might have actually been the motives of the two nations, the Khmer Rouge launched a series of armed attacks into Vietnamese territories first in April and then in June and July, and again in September. Such attacks clearly supplied Hanoi with new evidence of Phnom Penh's continuing intransigence and hostility, if not also its ever-growing collusion with China. The Vietnamese responded to all these attacks with determined, massive counter-offensives, and in fact by the summer had already gained the initiatives on the battlefronts by staging repeated operations into Kampuchean territory.[9] By virtue of their sheer scope, the Vietnamese offensives were in turn viewed by China as an outright bullying of a weaker nation, thereby pushing her even closer to Phnom Penh.

As the Vietnam-Kampuchea border conflict escalated into an almost full-scale war, the Sino-Vietnamese split over Kampuchea could no longer be concealed from public view. In face of the steadily growing military pressure exerted by Vietnam, Kampuchea in September rushed a high-powered delegation to China — the first one in two years — obviously to seek diplomatic support and military assistance. The delegation received an unusually warm welcome in Beijing with much publicity and pomp.[10] While the leaders of both countries delivered long speeches in each other's praises abounding with heavy revolutionary rhetoric, Hua Guofeng openly declared that China would "always stand with Kampuchea" in her "just struggle against imperialism and hegemonism".[11]

---

8. Hence the repeated Chinese declarations in late 1978 and early 1979 that China's restraint and forbearance had been mistaken for timidity and weakness by Vietnam. *XHNA*, December 12, 13, 24, 1978; February 11, March 8, 1979.
9. Heder, *op. cit.*, pp. 32–34.
10. *BR*, October 7, 1977, pp. 9–13.
11. *Ibid.*, p. 21.

In sharp contrast, when a Vietnamese delegation led by Le Duan visited Beijing on November 20, the reception it received was clearly businesslike and colourless. That Hanoi should have sent a delegation to Beijing in the middle of an escalating war with Kampuchea apparently reflected Vietnam's uncertainty about the extent of Chinese support for Phnom Penh and therefore her continuing hope for Beijing's sympathy towards her military action. As such, it was also a last attempt at least to dissuade China from open intervention and therefore to avert the final split. In fact, Le Duan during the visit reportedly asked China to use her influence with the Kampuchean government in order to reach a settlement, but Beijing flatly rejected the request and instead asked Vietnam to withdraw her troops from Kampuchea.[12] Whatever might have actually transpired in the meeting, it ended with no public mention whatsoever about the Kampuchean conflict, thereby suggesting differences between the two countries on the Indochina situation. In fact, China again made a veiled warning to Vietnam when Hua Guofeng in the presence of Le Duan openly reaffirmed Beijing's intention "to unite with the oppressed people and nations of the world ... and to ally with all countries subjected to imperialist and social-imperialist aggression, subversion, interference, control or bullying".[13]

The point of no return was reached in mid-December when Hanoi, apparently convinced of China's sympathy and support for Kampuchea and reassured of Soviet backing, launched a large-scale military operation across the border, with more than 50,000 troops supported by hundreds of armoured cars, artillery pieces and air cover, in a determined drive to convince Phnom Penh of Hanoi's military superiority. The military offensive led to Vietnamese occupation by the end of December of a 450-kilometre-long strip of Kampuchean territory stretching north to south, sometimes as much as twenty kilometres

---

12. *XHNA*, July 18, 1979. Also, *BR*, October 19, 1981, p. 27.
13. *BR*, November 25, 1977, pp. 5–8.

inside Kampuchea.[14] While the military operation represented
the climax of Vietnamese response to Kampuchean hostility and
was aimed at dealing a decisive blow to Kampuchean military
forces, in the eyes of Beijing it was a blatant display of
Vietnamese arrogance and certainly confirmed Hanoi's ambitions in Kampuchea. Although China still refrained from
accusing Vietnam openly, when Phnom Penh finally broke off
diplomatic relations with Hanoi on December 31, the Kampuchean Embassy in Beijing was provided with all the necessary
facilities to bring out its full charges against Vietnam, while
only excerpts of the official Vietnamese statement issued on
the same day on the border conflict were released to the press.
This clearly showed where Beijing's sympathy lay.[15] The
official pronouncements made by Vietnam and Kampuchea on
the border war also shed further light on the respective stands
and goals of the two countries in the conflict. While the Kampuchean statement contained only vehement attacks upon Vietnam's "systematic and large-scale aggressive acts of invasion"
and gave details of the territories encroached upon by Hanoi,[16]
the Vietnamese statement went to great lengths to capitalize
on the "unbreakable militant" solidarity and fraternal relationship" between Vietnam and Kampuchea fostered in "a long
struggle against colonialism lasting almost a century", which
had "bound the peoples of the two countries and the two communist parties of Vietnam and Kampuchea together".[17] Remin-

---

14. *FEER*, January 13, 1978, pp. 10–11; January 27, 1978, pp. 10–11;
    April 14, 1978, p. 39. *ST*, January 5, 1978, p. 3; January 17,
    1978, p. 12. The Khmer regime's charges were detailed in *BR*,
    January 6, 1978, p. 25. See also Heder, *op. cit.*, pp. 33–34.
15. *BR*, January 6, 1978, pp. 25–27; January 13, 1978, pp. 23–25.
    Also, *ST*, January 3, 1978, p. 1; January 10, 1978, p. 1. Vietnam
    actually protested over the handling of her statement in Beijing.
    ST, January 10, 1978, p. 1.
16. *BR*, January 6, 1978, pp. 25–26.
17. *MD*, January 4, 1978, pp. 6–8.

ding Kampuchea of the support and assistance Vietnam had given during the war years, Hanoi in fact contended that "both the immediate and long-term interests of the Vietnamese and Kampuchean peoples require that they continue to maintain such solidarity and friendship" which was meant to be "everlasting" and "unbreakable".[18] Similarly, on January 6, when Phnom Penh in another statement accused Hanoi of carrying out a "perfidious scheme to force Kampuchea to participate in its Indochina Federation" and demanded Hanoi to withdraw all its troops from Kampuchea so as to allow the Kampucheans "to live in full independence and sovereignty and to be masters of their own destiny",[19] Hanoi again reacted by dwelling extensively on the "bonds of solidarity and friendship" and the "special relationship" between Kampuchea and Vietnam which the Vietnamese "pledge their utmost efforts to defend and develop".[20]

That Vietnam should have continued to speak of solidarity and unity with Kampuchea — a theme to be repeated again and again — at a time when it had the least chance of realization and only after launching a massive invasion into Kampuchea, clearly revealed her paternalistic attitute towards the latter and her eagerness to see the emergence of a Kampuchea more accommodative to her wishes. Hanoi apparently calculated that its massive military thrust into Kampuchea had dealt sufficiently severe blows to Phnom Penh for it to come finally to a compromise with Vietnam. Thus, in early 1978, Hanoi launched an all-out peace campaign in what may be seen as a final attempt to pull Kampuchea back to Vietnam without resort to further use of force. In fact, in January alone, Vietnam on more than three occasions urged Kampuchea to negotiate with her to end the border conflict.[21] Hanoi even withdrew its

---

18. *Ibid.*, pp. 9–10.
19. *BR*, January 13, 1978, p. 24.
20. *MD*, January 12, 1978, pp. 6–8.
21. *Ibid.*, January 6, 1978, p. 13; January 12, 1978, p. 7; January

troops from major advancing positions in Kampuchea in order to promote an atmosphere congenial to peace talks.[22] On February 5, Hanoi made a formal proposal that called for a mutual withdrawal of forces to a line that was five kilometres behind their respective borders, to be followed by the conclusion of a treaty of friendship and non-aggression "on the basis of respect for each other's territorial sovereignty within the existing border".[23] The peace offer was repeated many times throughout the spring of 1978.[24] On April 7, to further dispel Kampuchea's fears, Hanoi issued a lengthy document entitled "On the Indochina Federation Question", in which it declared that the idea of an Indochina federation had "long passed into history" and that all that Hanoi desired was "to preserve and strengthen the militant solidarity and fraternal friendship" among the three Indochinese peoples.[25] As Hanoi explained the need for and nature of such a special relationship:[26]

> The history of 100 years of foreign domination experienced by the Indochinese peoples has proved that the imperialists, whether they were the French colonialists or the Japanese fascists, or the U.S. imperialists, all used Indochina as a

---

15, 1978, p. 18. *ST*, January 13, 1978, p. 1. As Hoang Tung, a high-ranking Vietnamese Party official, told Western reporters in April, the objective of Hanoi's military operation in December 1977 was "to deal a heavy blow to their [i.e., Kampuchean] divisions" and therefore to compel Kampuchea "to choose the other solution–negotiations". *FEER*, April 21, 1978, p. 18.

22. Hoang Nguyen, *The Vietnam-Kampuchea Conflict* (Hanoi: Foreign Languages Publishing House, 1979), p. 27. Phnom Penh also claimed that it had driven Vietnamese troops out of Kampuchea by January 6, 1978. *Radio Phnom Penh*, May 10, 1978.

23. *MD*, February 6, 1978, pp. 13–16.

24. *Ibid.*, April 8, 1978, p. 14; *VNA*, June 20, 1978; *RH*, May 19, 1978.

25. *MD*, April 8, 1978, p. 14.

26. *Kampuchea Dossier: I* (Hanoi: Foreign Languages Publishing House, 1978), p. 115; *MD*, April 8, 1978, pp. 14–15.

theatre of war, applied their traditional "divide-and-rule" policy, used one country as a springboard for aggression against another, and used one people to fight another, with the aim of conquering all the three countries. The solidarity of the peoples of the three countries against their common enemy was *an objective requirement* of the revolutionary cause of each people, a factor of decisive importance in winning victory in the national liberation struggle as well as in the *long-term* cause of national defence and construction carried out by each other.

Although Hanoi most probably did not expect much out of any peace talks that might be held, it apparently believed that if Kampuchea could be persuaded to return to the negotiating table, there would at least be a good chance of detaching her from China and therefore eventually attaining its own long-term goals in Kampuchea.

However, as it turned out, Vietnam's thinly-veiled paternalism towards Kampuchea and her stick-and-carrot strategy by their very nature and scope only further alarmed Kampuchea and China, both of which now considered Vietnam as bent on annexing Kampuchea. In fact, Hanoi's peace offers were accompanied by an intensified drive to foment popular revolt among the Khmer people in border provinces.[27] Thus, while Phnom Penh flatly rejected all the Vietnamese initiatives as deceitful and Hanoi's concept of "special relationship" as transparent guises for regional hegemony,[28] China also decided to drop all semblances of neutrality and to step up her military aid to Kampuchea in early 1978. In mid-January, a high-ranking

---

27. Hanoi began to call indirectly for the overthrow of the Pol Pot regime in late January of 1978. *RH*, January 27, 28, 1978. By March, Hanoi had already undertaken to organize a guerrilla movement against the Phnom Penh regime and lent military support to it. Heder, *op. cit.*, pp. 41–42, 46–47, 52–53.
28. Heder, *op. cit.*, pp. 41–42. Also, Sheldon Simon, "New Conflict in Indochina", *Problems of Communism*, September-October 1978, p. 31; *FEER*, April 21, 1978, p. 17.

government delegation led by Deng Yingchao, widow of the late Zhou Enlai, visited Kampuchea, apparently in a gesture of solidarity with Phnom Penh. While in Phnom Penh, Madam Deng declared: "The five principles of peaceful co-existence are the fundamental principles which must be adhered to by all countries of the world, including the socialist countries, in dealing with relations between the states".[29] When back in Beijing, Madam Deng reportedly told the visiting French Premier Raymond Barre: "From the Chinese point of view, Kampuchea has fallen victim to aggression by Vietnam".[30] In fact, Madam Deng's visit was accompanied by massive air and sea deliveries of arms and ammunition which were said to include long-range 130-mm and 150-mm artillery pieces and MIG-15 jet fighters.[31] A growing number of Chinese advisers were also sent to train Kampuchean soldiers to operate these weapons. On February 26, Hua Guofeng in his report to the Fifth National People's Congress obliquely said that "no country should seek hegemony in any region or impose its will on others". A few days later Vice Premier Deng Xiaoping hastened to point out that the country Hua had referred to was Vietnam.[32] These remarks were followed in early March by the dispatch of a Chinese technical mission of railway experts to Phnom Penh to repair and reconstruct Kampuchea's main railway line linking the capital with the country's only deep-water port at Kompong Som — the primary supply route for Chinese aid materials.[33] A radar-based anti-aircraft defence system was also supplied to Phnom Penh at the same time.[34] By early May, Kampuchean troops were reported to have for

29. *BR*, January 27, 1978, p. 4.
30. Nguyen, *op. cit.*, pp. 25–26.
31. *ST*, January 17, 1978, p. 12; *FEER*, March 17, 1978, p. 10; April 21, 1978, p. 19.
32. *FEER*, March 17, 1978, p. 11; *BR*, March 10, 1978, p. 37.
33. *ST*, March 7, 1978, p. 3.
34. Heder, *op. cit.*, p. 51.

the first time since 1975 put tanks and other armoured vehicles along with long-range guns into the war — an unmistakable sign of China's determination to help Kampuchea resist Vietnam.[35]

Although China's new posture did not yet represent a real change in her well-established policy towards Kampuchea nor the nature of her commitment to Phnom Penh, her increasingly open pro-Kampuchean stand along with the escalation of Chinese military assistance to Kampuchea at what Vietnam might have considered to be a delicate but crucial juncture of Vietnam-Kampuchea relations was in turn seen by Hanoi as clearly a deliberate act of sabotage against Hanoi's peace initiatives. What followed, therefore, was a chain of events in the spring of 1978 which led to a rapid deterioration of Sino-Vietnamese relations. Thus, in late February and early March, there was a sudden increase of high-level contacts between military leaders of the Soviet Union and Vietnam.[36] It was certainly no accident that in late March Hanoi launched a nationwide campaign against the ethnic Chinese in Vietnam, resulting in the exodus of 70,000 Chinese from Vietnam to China during the two months of April and May alone.[37] Although the campaign had its own origins, the timing and the magnitude of the mass exodus could not but give the impression that the Chinese in Vietnam had been deliberately singled out as a target of retaliation, at least in part, against China's support for Kampuchea. In fact, Hanoi claimed openly that

---

35. *ST*, May 19, 1978, p. 3.
36. Hanoi sent the commander of its Seventh Military Region bordering Kampuchea to the Soviet Union in early 1978 and a Soviet military delegation visiting Laos in February also held talks with Vietnam's military leaders. *FEER*, March 17, 1978, p. 10.
37. *BR*, August 18, 1978, p. 29. For a detailed analysis of the ethnic dispute, see Pao-min Chang, "The Sino-Vietnamese Dispute over the Ethnic Chinese", *The China Quarterly*, June 1982, pp. 195–230.

the exodus had been triggered by widespread rumours of impending war between China and Vietnam over Kampuchea.[38] By May, thousands of Chinese stripped of their property had reportedly been sent either to the "new economic zones" set up in remote border provinces to reclaim farm land or to the Kampuchean front to fight.[39] At about the same time, about 10,000 Chinese road builders in Laos were asked to leave the country, apparently at the behest of Hanoi.[40] That was not all. In June, Vietnam unilaterally suspended the Sino-Vietnamese Vice-Foreign Ministerial talks on territorial disputes that had been going on for ten months without any progress.[41] On June 30, Vietnam took the formal step to close ranks with the Soviet Union by announcing her admission to the COMECON.[42]

Whether Vietnam was still merely registering her anger or deliberately heightening the tension between China and herself, the escalation of Hanoi's anti-China propaganda and activities and its swing to alignment with Moscow clearly alerted Beijing to the extent to which Vietnam was prepared to go to alienate China. The expulsion of thousands upon thousands of ethnic Chinese into China, in particular, not only created serious economic and social problems for local Chinese authorities, but also immediately undermined the stability of the still disputed Sino-Vietnamese land border. Unable to resolve any bilateral differences through consultations and negotiations, and confronted with the continuing massive influx of refugees, Beijing also decided to toughen its stance and proceeded to exert direct pressure on Vietnam. On May 12, China cancelled twenty-one complete-factory aid projects to Vietnam and on May 30 scrapped another fifty-one similar

---

38. *MD*, May 28, 1978, p. 17; May 30, 1978, p. 22. Also *VNA*, May 27 and 31, 1978.
39. *ST*, May 4, 1978, p. 2; May 22, 1978, p. 3; May 30, 1978, p. 12.
40. *Ibid.*, June 16, 1978, p. 1.
41. *BR*, May 25, 1979, pp. 18, 20.
42. *ST*, June 30, 1978, p. 3.

projects.[43] Although the reason given for such measures was to divert urgently needed resources for the relief of refugees, they were clearly also designed as a political pressure on Vietnam. In fact, on June 5, only two days after receiving Ieng Sary, Kampuchea's Foreign Minister, Deng Xiaoping declared that China would take harsher measures against Vietnam if Hanoi persisted in its anti-China policy.[44] On June 5, China in what was intended to be at least a show of flag, declared unilaterally that she would dispatch ships to Vietnam to evacuate victimized Chinese residents. On June 16, Beijing shut down all the three Vietnamese consulates in China, and this was followed by the cancellation of all aids to Vietnam and the withdrawal of all Chinese technicians from that country on July 3.[45] On July 11, Beijing announced the closure of its land border with Vietnam.[46]

As the battle line between Vietnam and the Soviet Union on the one side and China and Kampuchea on the other was being clearly drawn, and as retaliatory measures and counter-measures were being adopted by Vietnam and China against each other, a war of words over the Kampuchean conflict also quickly came into the open. Thus, on May 25, the same day when Beijing first expressed its concern openly about the refugee crisis,[47] Hanoi already alluded to "international reactionaries who have great ambitions towards Southeast Asia and are attempting to sow division among the Vietnamese and Kampuchean peoples".[48] On June 5, Hanoi in a thinly-veiled attack on China attributed more specifically the continuing conflict between Kampuchea and Vietnam and particularly Phnom Penh's stubborn refusal to negotiate to "reactionary forces in this area...

---

43. *VNA*, June 17, 1978.
44. *XHNA*, June 5, 1978.
45 *Ibid.*, June 17, 1978; July 3, 1978.
46. *Ibid.*, July 11, 1978.
47. *Ibid.*, May 25, 1978.
48. *RH*, May 25, 1978.

whose interests cannot be reconciled . . . with the existence of a unified, independent and sovereign socialist Vietnam''.[49] On June 17, Hanoi finally came into the open and accused Beijing of having ''ceaselessly given all-round support to the Kampuchean authorities in launching their border war of aggression against the Vietnamese people . . . and in carrying out an anti-Vietnamese policy aimed at . . . sabotaging the tradition of solidarity and friendship between Vietnam and Kampuchea''.[50] In a series of statements that followed in late June and in July, Hanoi went a step further to attack, for the first time, the ''large-scale, systematic, ferocious, and barbaric genocide'' in Kampuchea and linked it to China's ambition in Southeast Asia.[51] Hanoi in fact claimed that the relations between the three communist parties in Indochina had been ''wonderfully pure until the Pol Pot-Ieng Sary clique usurped the leadership of the Kampuchean Communist Party and colluded with China'' in the late 1960s. From then on, the Pol Pot group became a ''cheap instrument'' of Beijing's strategy of expansion down to Southeast Asia.[52] Apparently referring to Vietnam's increasing drift away from China, Hanoi proceeded to identify the cause of Beijing's intervention in Kampuchean affairs: ''Vietnam has its independent and sovereign domestic and foreign policies which are not to the liking of China. That is why China tries to put pressure on Vietnam''.[53] And it was only by China's orders that the Pol Pot regime adopted a policy of genocide in Kampuchea and aggression against Vietnam, in order to destroy the Kampuchean race, thereby paving the way for China's conquest of other parts of Asia.[54] The Chinese were therefore held responsible for all the crimes committed against both the Kampuchean and Vietnamese peoples.

---

49. *Ibid.*, June 5, 1978.
50. *Ibid.*, June 17, 1978.
51. *VNA*, June 20, July 15, 1978.
52. *Ibid.*, June 20, July 15, 1978.
53. *RH*, August 1, 1978. See also, *VNA*, June 25, 27; July 6, 7, 1978.
54. *VNA*, June, 20, July 15, 1978.

Beijing was quick to respond to Hanoi's charges. On July 11, after the Sino-Vietnamese talks on the evacuation of Chinese from Vietnam had already been deadlocked, and on the eve of China's closure of her land border with Vietnam, *The People's Daily* published a long commentary in which Beijing openly accused Hanoi of first making an about-face in its position on the Vietnam-Kampuchea boundary issue and then waging a "naked war of aggression against Kampuchea ... in an attempt to subdue and gobble up Kampuchea by force".[55] Beijing charged that "victory in the war against U.S. imperialism, coupled with possession of great amounts of arms, has made the Vietnamese authorities' heads swell and their hands itch. They behave in a way as if Vietnam were a 'big power' ... and dream of rigging up an Indochina federation with Vietnam at its head".[56] In a follow-up commentary, China described Vietnam's "line of independence and sovereignty" as merely "a cover to encroach upon the independence and sovereignty of other countries"; Vietnam's concept of international solidarity also meant expecting others to "go along with them" and to "dance to their tune".[57] Beijing further claimed that only when Vietnam had failed in her "schemes of armed aggression and subversion against Kampuchea" did she "start venting her anger on China".[58] In fact, it was because "Vietnam considered China as a most formidable obstacle to the realization of her goal of regional hegemony" that Hanoi had to pursue an anti-China policy.[59] The Sino-Vietnamese territorial dispute, the expulsion of ethnic Chinese, and other anti-China manoeuvres were closely linked to the Kampuchean-Vietnamese border conflict, because all were parts of a plot in pursuit of hegemonism.[60] Moreover, China's suspicions of

---

55. *BR*, July 21, 1978, p. 6.
56. *Ibid.*, p. 8.
57. *Ibid.*, July 28, 1978, p. 28.
58. *Ibid.*, July 21, 1978, p. 6.
59. *Radio Beijing*, September 17, 1978.
60. *BR*, July 21, 1978, p. 6.

a Soviet-Vietnamese collaboration in Indochina were now openly expressed, as Beijing charged: "The Soviet superpower with its own hegemonistic aims provides cover and support for the Vietnamese authorities' regional hegemonism, while the Vietnamese authorities serve as a junior partner for the Soviet Union".[61] To show its unwavering stand on the Kampuchean conflict, Beijing reaffirmed its policy of "support and assistance to all just struggles against aggression as its bounden internationalist duty", and also warned that the "expansionist desires of Vietnam went far beyond Indochina".[62]

Although both the Vietnamese and Chinese charges must be viewed with some reservations, they did reveal the respective concerns of the two countries in Kampuchea. To the extent that China had all along been the principal and only ally of the Khmer regime, she could not have shirked the responsibility of strengthening a government not only hostile to Vietnam but also ruthless towards its own people. Indeed, without the political and material support of China, the Kampuchean regime would have found it difficult to persist in or sustain its anti-Vietnamese policy and activities.[63] And from the Vietnamese point of view, China's perennial interest in promoting an independent Kampuchea and thereby obstructing the renewal of the traditional solidarity and special relationship between Vietnam and Kampuchea could only reveal her own ulterior motives in the entire region. By capitalizing on the crimes of the Phnom Penh regime and by establishing a Chinese connection in both the internal and foreign policies of Kampuchea, Hanoi thus not only could shift the blame for the Kampuchean conflict squarely onto Beijing, but could also better justify any future and harsher actions it might be planning against Kampuchea.

---

61. *Ibid.*
62. *Ibid.*
63. This is also Hanoi's major argument. *Vietnam Courier*, March 1979, p. 16.

On the other hand, Vietnam's steadily mounting military and diplomatic pressures against Kampuchea since mid-1977 were apparently out of proportion to the nature and scope of the border conflict.[64] To the extent that such pressures were aimed at dealing fatal blows to the weaker Kampuchean armed forces and effecting a fundamental change in the character of the Kampuchean regime, they certainly smacked of big-powerism.[65] In the face of intense Kampuchean resistance to Vietnamese presence or influence and at a time of escalating hostilities between Phnom Penh and Hanoi, Hanoi's incessant affirmation of its traditional solidarity with Phnom Penh indeed sounded odd. Insofar as Vietnam had already succeeded in dominating Laos on the same premises, all the peace initiatives made towards Kampuchea did appear to be thinly disguised ruses for absorbing Kampuchea into a larger entity under Hanoi's control. And viewed in retrospect, Vietnam's drawn-out territorial and ethnic disputes with China and particularly her massive expulsion of the ethnic Chinese from Vietnam could hardly have been incidental to Vietnam's intentions in Kampuchea. From the Chinese point of view, therefore, Hanoi's persistent attempt to create a Kampuchea subservient to Vietnam and the extent to which it was prepared to go in order to attain its goal not only revealed its grand designs but also suggested instigation by an external power. Indeed, without Soviet political and military support, Hanoi would certainly have exercised greater self-restraint in dealing with either Kampuchea or China. By accusing Vietnam of blatant aggression and associating Hanoi's hegemonism with world-wide Soviet designs, Beijing thus sought to alert the international community to the broader implications of events in Indochina and also prove the righteousness of its own intervention in the conflict.

---

64. Heder, *op. cit.*, pp. 40–43, 52–53.
65. *Ibid.*, pp. 52–53.

Therefore, from July on, Sino-Vietnamese relations took a further turn for the worse as both sides intensified their preparations for a possible showdown over Kampuchea.[66] Convinced that trends in Kampuchea could not easily be reversed now with extensive Chinese involvement, Vietnam after July 1978 apparently decided to adopt a militant policy towards both China and Kampuchea. In fact, the fourth plenary session of the Vietnamese Communist Party Central Committee held in July passed a resolution which not only pinpointed China as Vietnam's immediate enemy, but also expressed Hanoi's "determination to rapidly win victory both politically and militarily in the southwestern border areas".[67] The immediate consequences were the launching of large-scale attacks by Vietnam in mid-June on the Kampuchean front, and the intensification of a propaganda drive in late June to foment popular uprisings among both the civilian population and army units of Kampuchea.[68] From July on, Vietnam in fact not only dropped all her proposals for negotiations but also began to move new army divisions from the north to the Kampuchean front, and deliberately escalated the border war by mounting for the first time sustained air attacks on Khmer positions, particularly in the Tay Ninh Province.[69] By late August, Vietnam had already occupied a long strip of territory in the provinces of Kompong Cham and Kratie, and as many as 16,000 Kampuchean troops

---

66. *FEER*, July 14, 1978, pp. 6–8.
67. Hoang Van Hoang's statement, in *BR*, September 7, 1979, p. 25. Also, *BR*, October 19, 1981, p. 27; *VNA*, July 18, 1979. The decision could have been made even earlier, i.e., in February 1978. *FEER*, February 23, 1979, pp. 33–34.
68. *FEER*, July 14, 1978, pp. 6–7; July 28, 1978, p. 27. *ST*, August 1, 1978, p. 1. In fact, Hanoi began to organize a Khmer guerrilla movement against Phnom Penh in March and openly called for the overthrow of the Pol Pot regime in April. Heder, *op. cit.*, pp. 52–53; *RH*, April 3, 1978.
69. *ST*, August 3, 1978, p. 2; *FEER*, August 3, 1978, p. 2; August 11, 1978, p. 10; Heder, *op. cit.*, pp. 59–60.

were already trapped in large-scale fighting in the Chup-Memot area.[70] In early October, Vietnam started to conduct battalion-sized sweeps into Kampuchea, leading to heavy fighting along the entire border.[71]

The steady escalation of Vietnamese pressure on Kampuchea was accompanied by the growing tension along the Sino-Vietnamese land border, as both sides were beefing up their military strength in preparation for possible wider armed conflict.[72] Starting with the first bloody skirmish on August 25, when dozens of Chinese and Vietnamese were killed or wounded, border incidents became increasingly numerous and violent.[73] By late September, accusations of territorial encroachments by army units were already made by both sides, leading to clashes of considerable scale.[74] Although China had certainly policed the increasingly chaotic land border with greater vigour as a result of the massive influx of ethnic Chinese from Vietnam, the scale and pattern of such incidents, as well as the nature and volume of the continuing exodus of Chinese from Vietnam, also suggested that Hanoi had somehow deliberately played up its dispute with Beijing, if only to draw Moscow closer to its side in a worsening conflict with China, and to obtain as much Soviet arms as possible for the impending invasion of Kampuchea.[75]

Indeed, it is no accident that in late August, Moscow began a massive airlift of military hardware to Hanoi which gave every sign of an emergency exercise, and also started equipping

---

70. *ST*, August 3, 1978, p. 2; August 29, 1978, p. 1. Also, Heder, *op. cit.*, pp. 59–60.
71. *ST*, October 19, 1978, pp. 1, 3; October 27, 1978, p. 36.
72. *FEER*, July 14, 1978, pp. 6–7.
73. *XHNA*, August 25, 1978; *VNA*, August 25, 1978.
74. *XHNA*, September 4, 1978; *BR*, September 29, 1978, p. 23. For Vietnamese charges, see *VNA*, September 12, 19, 22, 1978.
75. For a detailed analysis, see Chang Pao-min, "The Sino-Vietnamese Territorial Dispute", *Asia-Pacific Community*, Spring 1980, pp. 151–52.

Vietnamese bases along the Sino-Vietnamese border with offensive missiles aimed at China.[76] An additional 500 to 1,000 Soviet technicians and advisors were also sent to Vietnam during the summer, raising the total number of Soviet personnel to about 4,000 by mid-September.[77] Apart from the Soviet offer of a US$2.6 billion programme to beef up Vietnamese armaments and military installations, the COMECON countries agreed in early September to complete the construction of all projects to which China had ceased technical assistance.[78] In the month of September alone, in fact, the Soviet Union unloaded more military hardware in Vietnam than it had done in the entire previous year.[79] By mid-October, Moscow had already supplied Hanoi with the most advanced MIG-23 jet fighters which it had refused to give Vietnam at the height of the Vietnam War and still did not give some of its Warsaw Pact allies. Practically all such aircraft were reportedly stationed in the Gia Lam Airport north of Hanoi.[80] As Soviet weapons and advisors poured into Vietnam, Hanoi also felt more confident and less restrained in confronting China. It is thus no coincidence that the border tension reached a new peak during the last quarter of 1978 and particularly immediately before and after the conclusion of the Vietnamese-Soviet Treaty of Friendship and Cooperation on November 3.[81]

As Hanoi became increasingly militant towards both Kampuchea and China and moved closer to Moscow in the second half of 1978, Beijing also dropped all pretence of aloofness from Kampuchea. In fact, the manner in which Vietnam turned against China and the massive Soviet presence in Vietnam appeared to have supplied China with the conclusive evidence

---

76. *ST*, September 12, 1978, p. 2; December 15, 1978, p. 1.
77. *Ibid.*, October 27, 1978, p. 36.
78. *Ibid.*, September 12, 1978, p. 2; October 6, 1978, p. 3.
79. Heder, *op. cit.*, p. 60.
80. *BR*, November 24, 1978, p. 23.
81. Chang, "The Sino-Vietnamese Territorial Dispute", pp. 151–52.

of a joint Soviet-Vietnamese campaign against China. And precisely because of the unmistakable Soviet involvement in the Sino-Vietnamese conflict, Beijing felt all the more obligated to provide Phnom Penh with the necessary assistance in order to resist Vietnam, since Hanoi's Kampuchea policy now not only reflected its own ambitions in Indochina, but also represented a real Soviet threat to China's security which must be faced squarely. What China did or failed to do in Kampuchea could well tip the balance clearly in Soviet as well as Vietnamese favour. Thus, a series of exchanges of high-level delegations between the two countries starting in late July were invariably accompanied by China's open condemnations of Vietnamese aggression and her explicit pledges of "resolute support" for Kampuchea's "just struggle to uphold national independence and state sovereignty".[82] To bolster Phnom Penh's defence capability, China by late July had also sizeably stepped up her supply of military hardware and ammunition to Kampuchea, as shown in the sharp increase in both the number of Chinese transport aircraft going into Kampuchea and in the size of the Chinese military advisory group in the country.[83] By September, China was reported to be already training Kampuchean pilots to fly MIG-19 fighters and to have between 5,000 and 6,000 military advisors in Kampuchea.[84] As late as mid-December, an average of six Chinese freighters a month continued to unload their supplies at Kompong Som.[85] And according to Chinese diplomats, on the eve of the fall of Phnom Penh, China had delivered at least 200 tanks, 300 artillery pieces, 6 jet fighters and 2 bombers, as well as some naval vessels, in addition to large quantities of smaller weapons, and there were

---

82. *BR*, August 4, 1978, p. 3; September 15, 1978, p. 6; November 10, 1978, p. 4; December 15, 1978, p. 3; December 22, 1978, p. 15.
83. *FEER*, July 14, 1978, p. 7.
84. *Ibid.*, November 3, 1978, p. 15; *ST*, September 5, 1978, p. 28.
85. *FEER*, December 22, 1978, p. 18.

a total of 15,000 Chinese civilian and military technicians working in all fields in Kampuchea.[86] The final stage was set for a showdown between Vietnam and China over Kampuchea.

---

86. *ST*, May 2, 1979, p. 2.

4
The Double Invasions

If Vietnam's determination to step up her pressures on Kampuchea in the second half of 1978 had resulted in a further escalation of the drawn-out border war, Hanoi before October most probably considered an all-out invasion of Kampuchea as militarily unnecessary in addition to politically undesirable, particularly in view of the great disparity in military strength between the two countries.[1] Given the high posture China took on the issue of ethnic controversy throughout the summer and the firm support she expressed for Kampuchea, an outright, massive, and unrestrained military attack on Kampuchea could well also render the existing dispute with China explosive with unpredictable consequences. In fact, the Vietnamese strategy from early 1978 on had been to draw out the much smaller Kampuchean forces and pound them so as to chew them up, piece by piece, rather than to overrun the entire country or to occupy as much Kampuchean territory as possible.[2] Such well-

---

1. In early January 1978, Vietnam had about 615,000 men under arms, compared to Kampuchea's 90,000. The Vietnamese were also far superior to the Kampucheans in equipment and experience. *FEER*, January 13, 1978, pp. 14–15. By November, two-thirds of the Kampuchean troops, or 60,000, were stationed in eastern Kampuchea facing at least 100,000 Vietnamese troops across the border. *FEER*, November 3, 1978, p. 14; November 19, 1978, p. 12; December 22, 1978, p. 17.
2. *FEER*, April 21, 1978, p. 18; July 28, 1978, p. 27; November 3, 1978, pp. 14–15.

targeted military assaults were coupled with an intensified drive
to organize a Khmer resistance force among the 150,000 Kampuchean refugees in Vietnam.[3] Hanoi apparently calculated that
by a combination of internal mass uprising and external military
pressure, the Kampuchean regime would collapse relatively
rapidly.

However, by the end of the third quarter of 1978, the situation was rather different. Whatever fears Vietnam might have
had initially of China's possible reaction to a more militant Vietnamese posture in Kampuchea had largely dissipated. Beijing's
apparent acquiescence to the influx of over 160,000 refugees
and its failure to put an end to the continuing crisis had already
exposed China's glaring vulnerability vis-à-vis Vietnam.[4] The
absence of effective retaliation against Hanoi's repeated
challenges along the increasingly tense land border further
demonstrated China's timidity and powerlessness. It was quite
clear to Hanoi that if China had not been able or willing to
react forcefully to disputes which impinged immediately upon
her security and sovereignty, she would certainly be even less
capable of action over a conflict in a non-contiguous country
like Kampuchea. In fact, while proclaiming firm support for
Kampuchea, China as early as August already told Kampuchean
leaders that she would not be able to come to their help militarily
if Hanoi launched an all-out invasion.[5] If Vietnam still
had doubts about China's unwillingness or inability to intervene
effectively, she must have felt reassured by mid-October when
Deng Xiaoping said openly that although China would con-

---

3. *Ibid.*, July 28, 1978, pp. 26–27; November 3, 1978, p. 15. See
   also Stephen P. Heder, "The Kampuchean-Vietnamese Conflict," in David W.P. Elliott (ed.), *The Third Indochina Conflict*
   (Boulder: Westview Press, Inc., 1981), pp. 59–60.
4. Pao-min Chang, "The Sino-Vietnamese Dispute over the Ethnic
   Chinese", *The China Quarterly*, June 1982, pp. 213–18.
5. *FEER*, August 11, 1978, pp. 11–12; September 8, 1978, p. 12.
   Radio Phnom Penh, September 17, 1978.

tinue to support Kampuchea, she would not send her troops there.[6] On the other hand, the demand for greater military involvement on the part of Vietnam also steadily increased in the fall of 1978 due to her repeated failure either to stage a coup d'état in Phnom Penh or to develop a more or less viable and self-sustaining rebel movement, in spite of all the efforts made throughout the summer.[7] At the same time, the stubborn resistance put up by the Kampuchean forces in the third quarter of the year made the border war increasingly costly for Hanoi. In fact, without launching a frontal, massive assault on Kampuchea along the entire border, Vietnamese troops in isolated battles did not necessarily command much advantage in face of the hit-and-run tactics of the Kampuchean forces, particularly during the long rainy season.[8] The massive aid China was pouring into Kampuchea at an escalating rate throughout the third quarter of 1978 further reduced steadily the margin of Vietnam's military superiority in a semi-guerrilla warfare. And in view of the woeful domestic situation, certainly no Vietnamese leader cherished the prospect of fighting another long war of attrition.[9] By October, Vietnam had apparently come to believe that time was not on their side and a final massive offensive during the dry season was indispensable to an early and satisfactory conclusion of the Kampuchean war.

Perhaps a clear hint of Vietnam's growing inclination to execute a coup de grâce against Kampuchea was dropped in early September when Hoang Tung, Editor-in-Chief of the *Nhan Dan* and a senior member of the Vietnamese Communist Party, was indiscreet enough in an interview given to a French journalist to regret openly that Vietnam had not intervened in

---

6. *ST*, October 16, 1978, p. 3. Also, *FEER*, November 24, 1978, p. 10; January 12, 1979, p. 14, January 19, 1979, p. 12.
7. *FEER*, November 24, 1978, p. 12.
8. *Ibid.*, Novémber 19, 1978, p. 12. Also, *FEER*, January 19, 1979, p. 13.
9. *Ibid.*, August 4, 1978, p. 13.

Kampuchea in the early 1970s when large numbers of Vietnamese troops were stationed there. "If we had intervened, the situation would have evolved differently. . . . Perhaps we are paying for that mistake".[10] About the same time, foreign visitors to Hanoi were reportedly also told by Vietnamese officials that the Kampuchean regime " will not survive much longer" and that "it will be swept away before the end of the year".[11] It is perhaps no accident that starting in September, the Vietnamese media began to refer to a consolidated resistance movement operating on Kampuchean soil and openly placed Vietnam behind such a movement by calling repeatedly for the overthrow of the regime in Phnom Penh.[12] It was also during late September and early October that Hanoi began a massive military build-up along the entire Vietnam-Kampuchea border and beefed up its troop strength from 60,000–80,000 men to well over 100,000.[13] By mid-October, a combined general staff was already established in the province of Tay Ninh on the border, with Vietnamese troops moving into offensive positions in southern Laos as well, apparently in anticipation of the need to coordinate military activities on a large scale.[14]

However, while Vietnam's new, heightened military posture along the Kampuchean border clearly suggested Hanoi's preparedness to take bold initiatives in Kampuchea, and plans for an all-out invasion were most likely already being mapped out meticulously by October, it was clearly the conclusion of the Soviet-Vietnamese Treaty of Friendship and Cooperation on November 3 that gave the final green light for Hanoi to go ahead by removing whatever hesitation Vietnam might still have

---

10. *Agence France Presse*, Hanoi, September 7, 1978.
11. Reported by *Baltimore Sun* (U.S.A.) and quoted in *BR*, October 6, 1978, p. 36.
12. For instance, *RH*, September 9, 20, 1978.
13. *ST*, October 5, 1978, p. 30; October 7, 1978, p. 3; October 16, 1978, p. 3; October 23, 1978, p. 32; October 27, 1978, p. 36.
14. *Ibid.*, October 23, 1978, p. 32. Heder, *op. cit.*, p. 60.

in executing her plans.[15] Article Six of the Treaty specifically provided that in case either party was attacked or threatened with attack, the two parties signatory to the treaty would "immediately consult each other with a view to eliminating that threat", and would "take appropriate and effective measures to ensure the peace and the security of the two countries".[16] In view of the fact that no such treaty had existed when Vietnam was the object of attack by the United States and when her very survival was threatened, the document was clearly directed against China. That Vietnam should have needed such a symbol of alliance at a time when she had actually scored diplomatic victories on virtually all the disputes with China and was also under no apparent threat from Beijing militarily could only suggest that the treaty served the immediate if not the only purpose of removing all possibility of Chinese intervention following the anticipated Vietnamese invasion of Kampuchea.

The relative quietness on the battlefront throughout November after the announcement of the Soviet-Vietnamese Treaty, however, suggested that somehow Hanoi still hoped that the stepped-up military pressures or even the presence of an overwhelming war machine itself would be already sufficient either to break down finally the Kampuchean resistance on the battlefield or to induce internal rebellion that would bring down the Pol Pot regime, or both, without having to resort to the final act of outright invasion. It certainly indicated Hanoi's preoccupation with the organization of a presentable Khmer resistance movement that was still a necessity if only to serve as a spearhead of Vietnamese advance and therefore to justify an all-out Vietnamese assault upon Kampuchea. These considerations probably accounted for the sudden upsurge of reports from Hanoi on armed uprisings in eastern and

---

15. *Vietnam Courier*, December 1978, pp. 3–5; *FEER*, December 22, 1978, p. 17.
16. *Vietnam Courier*, December 1978, p. 5.

southeastern Kampuchea throughout October and November.[17] They also explained the fact that as late as the end of November, Hanoi continued to confine its military actions to the rural border areas and refrained from penetrating deep along the main highways into Kampuchean territory.[18] As a result, Western analysts until mid-December remained somewhat puzzled at the intentions of Hanoi and even ruled out a massive invasion against Kampuchea.[19]

The announcement on December 3 of the establishment of the Kampuchean National Front for National Salvation (KNFNS), with a complete list of leading personalities and an elaborate set of programmes on both internal and external policies of a new Kampuchea, therefore clearly foreshadowed what was forthcoming. With the explicit aim of overthrowing the Pol Pot regime, and professing support from "millions" of Kampucheans, it also paved the way for a rapid escalation of the fighting without further constraints on the part of the Vietnamese.[20] It was indeed no coincidence that no sooner had the KNFNS come into existence than the Vietnamese along with Hanoi-backed Kampuchean insurgent units began to penetrate deep into Kampuchean territory along the entire border.[21] By mid-December, the Vietnamese troops had reportedly already consolidated their positions in the entire Parrot's Beak and Fish Hook regions and were closing in on the Mekong cities of Kratie and Kompong Cham, both lying as far as fifty miles inside Kampuchea.[22] Nevertheless, the Kampuchean forces apparently

---

17. *ST*, October 23, 1978, p. 3; October 24, 1978, p. 3; October 25, 1978, p. 3. *RH*, November 15, 1978. *VNA*, November 24, 1978. *FEER*, November 24, 1978, p. 12.
18. *FEER*, November 3, 1978, p. 14; November 24, 1978, p. 12.
19. *Ibid.*, November 3, 1978, p. 14; November 24, 1978, p. 12.
20. *Sapordamean Kampuchea* (Kampuchean News Agency) (Phnom Penh), December 3, 4, 15, 1978.
21. *ST*, December 8, 1978, p. 40; *FEER*, December 15, 1978, p. 34.
22. *FEER*, December 22, 1978, p. 17.

adopted a strategy of stubborn resistance as long as Vietnam held back her main units. And as the battleline was being quickly stretched, the strength of the insurgents and the level of Vietnamese troops already committed became increasingly inadequate. In order to take advantage of the dry season and bring the war to an end as soon as possible, Hanoi on December 25 launched a swift, high-profile, and all-out invasion when more than 100,000 Vietnamese troops backed by war planes, tanks and artillery began to roll into Kampuchea along the main highways. From then on, there was little resistance from the Kampuchean forces, which simply melted away into the forests and mountains.[23] Twelve days later, on January 6, 1979, Phnom Penh fell almost without a fight.

It is perhaps significant that in reporting on the large-scale offensive from early December on, Hanoi made no link between its military drive and China's threat to Vietnam. The military operation was invariably described as a "war of liberation" or "people's struggle" waged by the newly established National Front in support of the uprisings of the Kampuchean people, and the immediate objective was "to eliminate the genocidal Pol Pot-Ieng Sary clique and to bring an end to the Vietnam-Kampuchea border war".[24] In fact, throughout the final twelve-day Vietnamese penetration into Kampuchea, Hanoi was conspicuously silent on the entire Kampuchean situation and did not mention a single word about either Vietnam's own role in the entire operation or China's threat by way of Kampuchea. Only after the capture of Phnom Penh did Hanoi admit that it had launched "counter-attacks" to repulse the Pol Pot regime's "territorial encroachments".[25] And in greeting the victory, Radio Hanoi merely declared that the developments in Kampuchea had eliminated the cause of conflict between

23. *ST*, May 4, 1979, p. 16.
24. *Sapordamean Kampuchea*, December 3, 4, 15, 1978. *RH*, December 24, 31, 1978.
25. *VNA*, January 6, 1979; *RH*, January 13, 1979.

Kampuchea and her neighbours, thereby "paving the way for peace and stability" in the region.[26]

If Vietnam's reluctance to implicate China was due mainly to her presumed neutrality in the entire Kampuchean operation, it did not take long for Hanoi to reveal its real motivation in undertaking such an operation. On January 7, 1979, the Party newspaper *Nhan Dan* hailed the capture of Phnom Penh as "having ushered in a new era in Indochina" and hastened to place Kampuchea in proper context by declaring: "From now on the three fraternal nations — Vietnam, Kampuchea, and Laos, will unite with one another to build a new life.... This strong solidarity constitutes a strength which no force can destroy".[27] Such solidarity took on concrete form on February 16, merely one month after Hanoi had installed the Heng Samrin regime, when Hanoi's Prime Minister Pham Van Dong flew to Phnom Penh to conclude a Treaty of Peace, Friendship and Cooperation with the new Kampuchean government. The document turned out to be very similar to that signed between Vietnam and Laos in July 1977. While stressing the need for "all-round cooperation" between Vietnam and Kampuchea, the treaty repeatedly mentioned the "tradition of militant solidarity and fraternal friendship" between the two countries and obligated the two parties to "preserve the purity" of such solidarity and friendship. Moreover, like the Vietnam-Laos Treaty, the Vietnam-Kampuchea Treaty was also to be valid for twenty-five years and would be automatically renewed thereafter for successive periods of ten years unless one party intended to cancel it.[28] It was further supplemented by two other bilateral agreements on cooperation in practically all aspects of life.[29] On February 23, the *Nhan Dan* already openly proposed the creation of an "Indochinese union" consisting

---

26. *RH*, January 9, 11, 1979. *FEER*, January 26, 1979, p. 11.
27. *RH*, January 7, 8, 1979.
28. *Vietnam Courier*, March 1979, pp. 5–6.
29. *VNA*, February 16–18, 1979.

of Vietnam, Laos and Kampuchea, and claimed that the "militant solidarity and fraternal friendship" between the three nations constituted "a necessary objective and a *law* in the development of the revolution in each country".[30] A Vietnam-dominated Indochina finally dawned.

The high profile in which Vietnam had moved into Kampuchea and the speed at which she formalized her special relationship with that country clearly astonished China. If by November 1978 Vietnam had planned for an invasion but still hesitated to execute it, China certainly had not expected it to occur at all, much less to be prepared to respond in kind.[31] As a matter of fact, in aiding a distant and weak Kampuchea against her bigger neighbour, Beijing was fully aware of its own limitations. While Vietnam needed only to buttress her military superiority and to buy political insurance from the Soviet Union to ensure a successful campaign against Kampuchea, China had to make an all-out effort merely to keep the Phnom Penh regime afloat. Apart from the difficulties involved in supplying a non-contiguous country, the main problem China faced in Kampuchea was to turn — in a matter of months, if not weeks — a small guerrilla army into a relatively modern combat force capable of handling heavy artillery, tanks, and aircraft, in order to withstand the might of not only much larger but also far better equipped Vietnamese forces. And the difficulties proved to be insurmountable, particularly in view of the still fanatically nationalistic orientation of the Pol Pot regime and the extreme shortage of skilled personnel after the extensive purges of 1975–77.[32] Yet even if everything had gone well, the

---

30. *ST*, February 24, 1979, p. 36.
31. That China did not expect Phnom Penh to fall so fast or at least was not prepared for it was further underscored by the haste and disorder in which Chinese diplomats and technicians were evacuated in early January, some of them even on foot. *FEER*, January 19, 1979, p. 11; *ST*, May 2, 1979, p. 2.
32. Chinese diplomats arriving in Bangkok from Phnom Penh were

disparity in power between Vietnam and Kampuchea would have been still such that, short of China fighting the war on behalf of Kampuchea, which was clearly out of the question, Phnom Penh could not have emerged a credible match for Vietnam in an all-out military confrontation, no matter how much aid Beijing was able to provide.

Consequently, although China throughout the second half of 1978 never wavered in her diplomatic support to Kampuchea and also tried her best to boost the Kampuchean defence capabilities, Beijing apparently hoped that the staunch verbal Chinese support plus a massive Chinese presence in Kampuchea would be sufficient to deter an all-out Vietnamese assault, for that could only mean direct confrontation between Vietnam and China.[33] In fact, the whole policy of China's propping up Kampuchea militarily was based upon the assumption that Vietnam at least would not openly commit an act of massive aggression against Kampuchea in the purview of the international community. And as long as no large-scale invasion took place, it was entirely feasible for the Kampuchean forces to confine Hanoi's territorial ambitions within limited bounds.

Therefore, in spite of all the help extended to Kampuchea, China betrayed a clear anxiety to reduce the chances of an all-out war between Vietnam and Kampuchea, particularly in the last quarter of 1978 when the shadow of a large-scale Vietnamese invasion was actually growing. In fact, Beijing's declaration in August that she would not send troops to Kampuchea was not merely a recognition of hard reality but also somehow aimed at reminding Phnom Penh of the limited nature of Chinese commitment and conveying to Hanoi China's modest goals in Kampuchea.[34] Even after the signing of the Soviet-

---

frank enough to complain in great detail about the misuse of Chinese aid materials and the difficulties in implementing China's aid programmes. See *ST*, May 2, 1979, p. 2.

33. See Heder, *op. cit.*, pp. 50–51.
34. *Ibid.*, p. 58.

Vietnamese Treaty in early November, which apparently confirmed China's worst fears, Beijing's attitude remained cautious.[35] A high-level Chinese delegation dispatched to Phnom Penh immediately after the announcement of the Soviet-Vietnamese treaty did little more than advise Kampuchea to be prepared to give up the capital if necessary and to fight a "protracted guerrilla war" in the countryside.[36] In mid-November, Deng Xiaoping even openly predicted the fall of Phnom Penh without, however, suggesting or threatening any measures of retaliation.[37] In fact, it was precisely China's reluctance or rather inability to commit herself fully to the defence of Kampuchea that had compelled Phnom Penh to propose, with Chinese encouragement and endorsement, in early October and again in early November, to sign "immediately in Phnom Penh, Hanoi, or any other place a treaty of friendship and non-aggression" with Vietnam if only Hanoi would stop its military actions against Kampuchea.[38] Having received no response from Hanoi, Kampuchea in what appeared to be a desperate move to avert the unpleasant eventuality, actually had to make an open appeal in late November to "all friendly nations" for emergency assistance in order to keep Vietnam out.[39]

That Vietnam should have launched the invasion at all in such a blatant manner not only shattered all Beijing's hopes for containing the scope of the conflict, but also constituted

---

35. In early November, Deng Xiaoping said that Chinese reaction to the Soviet-Vietnamese Treaty "would depend on the moves by Vietnam. . . . First, we must watch and see how much aggression they make against Kampuchea. Then we will decide about measures that we will take". China was thus still unsure of the Vietnamese intentions. *ST*, November 9, 1978, p. 28.
36. *FEER*, November 24, 1978, p. 11. Also, December 15, 1978, p. 34; January 12, 1979, p. 14.
37. *Ibid.*, November 24, 1978, p. 10
38. *BR*, October 13, 1978, p. 21; November 10, 1978, p. 4.
39. The message was carried in *XHNA*, December 6, 1978.

politically a severe and humiliating blow to China, since it made a big mockery of the resolute support — both in words and in deeds — which Beijing had vehemently proclaimed and repeatedly demonstrated for Kampuchea. Insofar as Hanoi's decision to overrun the entire Kampuchea militarily was made on the presumption of powerful Soviet backing and Chinese impotence and timidity, the invasion also posed a direct and immediate challenge to China's stature and power, to which Beijing now had no choice but to respond. After all the fruitless tussles and wrangles over other bilateral issues of dispute, to allow Vietnam to have her way in Kampuchea would in fact be tantamount to a total surrender of China to Vietnam. It would certainly encourage Vietnam to launch more territorial adventures against China and expel more Chinese from Vietnam. Thus, even though China could not have expected to reverse the situation in Kampuchea, something had to be done, if only to take off some of the Vietnamese pressures on the retreating Khmer forces, and to restore Beijing's own credibility which had been already severely eroded in the eyes of all. To the extent that the Vietnamese invasion made a Chinese military response now more justifiable than the case would otherwise be, it certainly also removed the political constraints on China's use of force against Vietnam.

But that was not all. To the degree that the Vietnamese invasion had been actually backed by the Soviet Union materially and diplomatically, it not only once again confirmed Beijing's fears of a Soviet-Vietnamese scheme to contain China from the south, but also alerted Beijing to the scope of Soviet ambitions in Indochina and the extent to which Moscow was determined to pursue its objectives. It was therefore the blatant manner in which Hanoi had gone into Kampuchea and in which Moscow had supported Vietnam's military adventure that China found particularly worrisome and unacceptable. And from the Chinese point of view, to arrest Vietnamese aggression in Indochina was in fact to contain Soviet ambitions in Southeast Asia. If Vietnam was not stopped in Kampuchea and if China continued to convey an impression of timidity and impotence, she might well face a more grave threat from Moscow by encouraging Soviet adventures not only in China's southern flank, but also along her long but poorly defined northern border.

Moreover, the Vietnamese invasion of Kampuchea did not only provide the crucial catalyst for China's decision to intervene militarily, but also determined the scale of such intervention. Although before February 1979 some form of punitive action against Vietnam might well have already been planned and executed if only to ensure minimum peace and order along the increasingly chaotic Sino-Vietnamese border,[40] a large-scale invasion across the border was clearly not what China had originally envisaged. Yet after the massive Vietnamese invasion, it became quite clear that unless a military operation of a similar scope was launched against Vietnam, China could not have expected to demonstrate her determination to confront Vietnam militarily and to obstruct Soviet advance in Indochina. Nor could she have expected to slow down the Vietnamese conquest of Kampuchea.

That China's decision to launch a massive attack upon Vietnam was made only after the Vietnamese invasion had occurred was amply shown in the sharp differences in her attitudes and actions between the two periods demarcated by December 25. In fact, Chinese protests and warnings to Vietnam made before that date were either mild in tone or vague in implications, and did not go beyond Beijing's immediate concern about territorial encroachments and stability along the Sino-Vietnamese border. And as late as mid-December, when Vietnam was all set to move into Kampuchea, there was still no sign of a corresponding Chinese build-up in the border area apart from increased reconnaissance flights.[41] All this apparently accounted for the long lapse of forty days between the Vietnamese invasion of Kampuchea and the Chinese invasion

---

40. *FEER*, November 24, 1978, pp. 10–11.
41. *Ibid.*, December 22, 1978, p. 17.

of Vietnam. It also explained, at least in part, the "supreme confidence" expressed by Hanoi in Beijing's non-intervention even up to the eve of the Chinese invasion, as well as the fact that Vietnamese forces stationed along the Sino-Vietnamese border were both limited in quantity and somewhat irregular in character.[42] Yet on December 24, 1978, on the eve of the Vietnamese invasion of Kampuchea, China in two successive statements issued in one day delivered the hitherto most piercing verbal attack on Vietnam when she declared:[43]

> Vietnam has gone far enough in pursuing her anti-China course. There is a limit to the Chinese people's forbearance and restraint. China has never bullied and will never bully any other country; neither will it allow itself to be bullied by others. It will never attack unless it is attacked. But if it is attacked, it will certainly counter-attack. China means what it says. We wish to warn the Vietnamese authorities that if they, emboldened by Moscow's support, try to seek a foot after gaining an inch and continue to act in this unbridled fashion, they will decidedly meet with the punishment they deserve. We state this here and now. Do not complain later that we've not given you a clear warning in advance.

Although the statements were apparently made in response to the escalation of violent incidents along the Sino-Vietnamese land border, it was clearly also intended to be a general warning to Vietnam on other matters. The unusual phraseology of the statements was certainly revealing enough of China's changing dispositions in her drawn-out conflict with Vietnam.

Indeed, it was only in early January of 1979 that Western intelligence sources began to monitor a "massive and hasty" build-up of enormous amounts of armour and artillery along China's border with Vietnam which signified a possible Chinese

---

42. *Ibid.* Foreign analysts as late as mid-January doubted that China would launch a sustained offensive against Vietnam. *The New York Times*, January 22, 1979, p. 3.
43. *BR*, December 29, 1978, pp. 24–25.

invasion on a large-scale.[44] However, not until Phnom Penh had fallen to the Vietnamese did China begin to relate their threatening remarks specifically to the Vietnamese invasion of Kampuchea. The first clear hint that China might launch a large-scale military operation against Vietnam was dropped on January 8 by a high-ranking official at the People's Institute of Foreign Affairs in Beijing, when he told a group of visiting U.S. senators accompanied by Ambassador Woodcock: "The Vietnamese are crazy. They believe they have defeated the French and the Americans and now the Kampucheans, and now they think they can defeat China. They must be taught a lesson. There will be a war".[45] On January 29, Deng Xiaoping while confirming unusual Chinese troop movements, told the U.S. Senate in Washington: "We cannot allow Vietnam to run wild everywhere. . . . We may be forced to do what we do not like to do. . . . Vietnam must be taught some necessary lessons".[46] The same warning was repeated by Deng in Tokyo on February 7 on his way back to Beijing, when he told the Japanese Prime Minister explicitly that "Vietnam must be punished for its action [in Kampuchea]", for "if we remain inactive, the military action [in Kampuchea] might spread to ASEAN".[47] It was also no accident that only in early February, when China had concentrated 160,000 regular troops, 700 aircraft, and hundreds of heavy artillery pieces along the Vietnamese border, did Hanoi take the threat seriously by hastily transferring a number of MIG-21 fighters from its hard-pressed southern command to the north and by adding a new missile-launching site to its border defence network.[48]

During the Chinese invasion that began on February 16, Beijing also did not hesitate to link its military action to the

---

44. *ST*, January 7, 1979, p. 2; May 4, 1979, p. 16. *FEER*, January 12, 1979, p. 14; February 16, 1979, p. 10.
45. *ST*, May 4, 1979, p. 16.
46. *The New York Times*, January 31, 1979.
47. *XHNA*, February 7-8, 1979. Also, *ST*, February 8, 1979, p. 1.
48. *FEER*, February 16, 1979, p. 10.

Kampuchean situation. It was perhaps no coincidence that the all-out attack was launched on the same day when Pham Van Dong arrived in Phnom Penh to sign the Kampuchean-Vietnamese Treaty that laid the legal basis for a Hanoi-dominated Indochina.[49] On February 24, at a United Nations Security Council meeting on the Sino-Vietnamese border war, the Chinese delegate, after declaring that the objectives of China's military action were limited, urged the Security Council to take "immediate and effective measures to stop Vietnam's armed aggression against Kampuchea and to bring an end to Vietnam's military occupation of Kampuchea".[50] Two days later, Deng Xiaoping responding to a query of a journalist openly said that "one should first ask why Vietnamese troops entered Kampuchea" before asking when China's lesson would end. He also reiterated that "China could not tolerate the Cuba of the Orient [i.e., Vietnam] to go swashbuckling in Laos, Kampuchea or even on the Chinese border".[51] Throughout the one-month operation, the Chinese media also did not hesitate to describe the aim of Chinese intervention as "nipping in the bud" any plan for a "greater Vietnam" or "Indochinese federation".[52] The punitive nature of the Chinese invasion was also made clear by China's repeated declarations during the military operation that the purpose of the Chinese action was to "destroy the myth that Vietnam is the third largest military

---

49. In a note sent to the president of the Security Council on February 15, the eve of the Chinese invasion, China already urged the United Nations to take necessary actions so that the Vietnamese would not only "halt their armed incursions and provocations against China", but also "withdraw all their forces from Kampuchea". *XHNA*, February 16, 1979.
50. *Renmin Ribao* (People's Daily) (Beijing), February 26, 1979, p. 5. Also, *BR*, March 2, 1979, p. 19.
51. *XHNA*, February 27, 1979.
52. *Renmin Ribao*, February 18, 1979, p. 1; February 19, 1979, p. 6; March 1, 1979, p. 5. *ST*, March 22, 1979, p. 3.

power and therefore could do anything it wants".[53] After China's military objectives had been attained in early March, Beijing once again proclaimed: "Those who worship armed forces only understand one language — that of armed forces. The Vietnamese authorities had for thousands of times shown off armed strength, created myths of 'a hundred battles, a hundred victories' and 'the third military power'. . . . Restraint and forbearance on the part of China were taken for invitation to more bullying. The Chinese border troops under these circumstances were driven beyond forbearance and launched counter-attack. They are determined to repulse this rampant 'third military power'. After sixteen days of counter-attack, these [Vietnamese] myths have been exploded".[54]

However, the Chinese invasion did not have Kampuchea and Vietnam as the only targets but also served the larger purpose of containing the expanding Soviet influence in Indochina or at least expressing Chinese determination to confront the Soviet threat squarely. This was quite evident in China's contingency plan made in connection with her invasion. On February 16, just before China launched the attack, Vice Premier Deng Xiaoping at a high-level Party conference analysed in some detail possible Soviet reactions to the Chinese invasion of Vietnam and said: "We have long ago made full preparations for a Soviet invasion. If they attack on a big scale, we shall fight them on a big scale; if they attack on a medium scale, we shall fight them on a medium scale; and if they attack on a small scale, we shall fight them on a small scale".[55] During the Chinese invasion, Deng also said publicly that China was prepared for a possible war with the Soviet Union.[56] As a matter of fact, in order to cope with a possible Soviet invasion,

---

53. *XHNA*, February 27, March 7, 1979.
54. *Ibid.*, March 8, 1979.
55. Reported in *Ming Bao* (Hong Kong), March 4, 1979, p. 1.
56. *Kyodo News Agency*, Tokyo, February 26, 1979; *Agence France Presse*, February 27, 1979. *ST*, February 28, 1979, p. 1.

China in early February of 1979 had put her troops along the Sino-Soviet border on an emergency war footing, set up a new military command in the remote Xingjiang Autonomous Region, and even evacuated 300,000 civilians from the exposed areas along the border.[57] And Chinese leaders after the war were frank enough to admit that "a lesson for Vietnam is also a lesson for the Soviet Union".[58]

Although executed only at a considerable cost to herself, China did accomplish a number of limited objectives with her invasion of Vietnam. As it was a move almost totally unexpected by Vietnam, the one-month-long operation was a timely reminder to Hanoi of China's potential impact as a bigger neighbour, her preponderant weight in regional affairs, and her capability for military action. The fact that the invasion had taken place in disregard of the newly formed Soviet-Vietnamese alliance and the ominous presence of a Soviet fleet off Vietnam also demonstrated, though perhaps belatedly, the extent to which Beijing was prepared to go in order to contain Hanoi's regional ambitions. By inflicting substantial casualties and damages upon Vietnam, China did deal a major blow to Hanoi's military forces and its entire defence network along the northern border.[59] By giving the retreating Khmer forces a breathing spell and a boost in morale, the Chinese invasion also had the immediate effect of slowing down the Vietnamese offensive in Kampuchea, if only temporarily. Although Chinese troops were soon withdrawn back to Chinese territory, their

---

57. *ST*, February 6, 1979, p. 28; February 13, 1979, p. 2; February 22, 1979, pp. 1, 26. *The New York Times*, February 12, 1979, p. 7.
58. *ST*, March 6, 1979, p. 1.
59. Casualties in the Sino-Vietnamese border war were estimated to be around 50,000 killed or wounded for Vietnam and 20,000 for China. *The New York Times*, May 3, 1979, p. 1. See also H.W. Jencks, "China's Punitive War on Vietnam: A Military Assessment", *Asian Survey*, August 1979, pp. 801–15.

continuing presence along the Vietnamese border was sufficient to constitute a looming shadow and a real threat to Vietnam which now had to be reckoned with. It certainly began to tie down a considerable proportion of Vietnamese troops that would otherwise be made available in Kampuchea.

However, as far as the Sino-Vietnamese conflict in general and the Kampuchean war in particular were concerned, the Chinese invasion did not really contribute to their solutions, since it added an emotional dimension to a drawn-out quarrel between China and Vietnam without actually altering the existing balance of forces in Kampuchea. Having demonstrated Beijing's objection to Hanoi's military action in Kampuchea in a most unambiguous and forceful manner, China was now also inadvertently and inextricably entangling herself with the Khmer Rouge which Vietnam had been determined to defeat and destroy. Yet as China was both unwilling and unable to prolong her military operation in Vietnam, the one-month-long invasion could not have persuaded Vietnam of the need to abandon her Kampuchea policy or begun to roll back the Vietnamese occupation of Kampuchea. In fact, precisely because of its explicitly "punitive" character, the Chinese invasion may well have made Hanoi more determined than ever to stay in Kampuchea, for to do otherwise could only imply Hanoi's submission to Beijing's demands under the sheer pressure of force. Indeed, by lending the hitherto most plausible credence to Vietnam's claim that the Pol Pot regime was merely a puppet of China and a tool of Chinese expansionism, the Chinese military action in a way provided Vietnam with an ideal pretext for holding on to Kampuchea and proceeding with her conquest.

5
Between Peace and War

In retrospect, the brevity of the Chinese invasion, its deliberately limited objectives, and the repeated public Chinese assurances of them,[1] suggested that the entire operation was intended mainly to serve a larger political purpose. By administering a major military lesson to Vietnam without, however, shutting completely the doors to negotiations, Beijing apparently hoped to arrest Vietnam's continuing drift away from China, if not actually drawing her back to the Chinese side. That China was more eager than Vietnam to negotiate a settlement was evident not only in the fact that Beijing initiated the new round of peace talks after the war and proposed it three times even before the hostilities ended,[2] but also in the conciliatory tone of her

---

1. When launching the invasion, China declared repeatedly that the operation was no more than a lesson to Vietnam, that China did not want a single inch of Vietnamese territory, and that her troops would be withdrawn when her objectives were accomplished. *XHNA*, February 17, 26, 1979. *Agence France Presse*, Hong Kong, February 19, 23, 27, 1979. *Kyodo News Agency*, Tokyo, February 26, 1979. In spite of Hanoi's exaggerations of the objectives and scope of the Chinese attack, only 75,000–85,000 Chinese troops out of a total of about 225,000 stationed along the border crossed into Vietnam. *Agence France Presse*, Hong Kong, February 27, 1979. Also, the military operation was confined to four centres of communication, and except in the remote Lai Chau Province, Chinese troops never advanced beyond 25 miles from the border. *FEER*, March 9, 1979, pp. 13–14.
2. *XHNA*, February 17, 26; March 1, 5, 1979.

diplomacy immediately after the war. Thus, Han Nianlong, the Chinese chief delegate, at the first session of the first round of talks in fact made an earnest appeal to Vietnam to take to heart the traditional ties between the two countries. Describing China and Vietnam as "sharing weal and woe, and supporting and helping one another in the long years of revolutionary struggle", Han reminded Vietnam that the "profound friendship" between the two countries was "nurtured on the blood of Chinese and Vietnamese revolutionaries and based upon the true mutual affection of the two peoples".[3] Without mentioning Kampuchea specifically, Han proceeded: "Facts show that it is in the fundamental interests of the Chinese and Vietnamese peoples and beneficial to the cause of peace and stability in Southeast Asia and in Asia to uphold and strengthen this friendship".[4] Deploring the rapid deterioration of Sino-Vietnamese relations in recent years in spite of China's "painstaking efforts" to avoid it, Han declared that China did not want to seek hegemony nor act as a superpower, but was merely opposed to the "hegemonistic designs of superpowers" and the bullying of small countries by big countries. It was only because Vietnam had "pursued an expansionist foreign policy ... ignored China's admonishments repeatedly, kept sending more and more troops to the Sino-Vietnamese border, and escalated their armed incursion into China" that the Chinese side was "compelled to take the kind of action which it did not wish to take", and "reluctantly launched its counter-attack in self-defence".[5] Assuring Vietnam that China was in the process of striving for socialist modernization and needed an "international environment of peace and stability", the Chinese delegation expressed the hope that Vietnam would "cherish as much as we do the traditional friendship" between the two

---

3. *Ibid.*, April 18, 1979.
4. *Ibid.*
5. *Ibid.* See also *XHNA*, April 26, July 18, 1979; *BR*, May 11, 1979, p. 19.

countries and was even confident that if Hanoi was serious about the negotiations, it would not be difficult to settle the dispute between the two countries after only one round of talks.[6]

In fact, throughout the peace talks lasting for over one year, Beijing dwelt repeatedly and painstakingly on the nature and extent of political and material support China had rendered Vietnam and the magnitude of sacrifices she had made for Vietnam during the two Indochina wars.[7] In particular, Beijing took the trouble of recalling in great detail how China had stood behind Vietnam unswervingly as the lone ally during the 1950s and 1960s, how an intimate relationship between the two countries had been manifested during Ho Chi Minh's times, how China had economized in order to supply Vietnam with scarce materials and equipments, and how thousands of Chinese personnel had risked their lives in keeping the communication lines between the two countries open and had helped with and actually died in the defence of North Vietnam during the intensive American bombing and naval blockade.[8] At the same time, Beijing also enumerated in detail how China had always striven to seek a reasonable settlement of all the bilateral disputes and exercised self-restraint when the relations deteriorated in the late 1970s, and how Vietnam had, on the other hand, returned evil for good by "intensifying her opposition and hostility to China" and by "widening the differences and aggravating tension". Proclaiming openly her "great pain and sorrow" over Vietnam's anti-China stance and activities, China nevertheless repeatedly expressed her hope that Vietnam would "set store by the traditional friendship and fundamental interests of the two peoples" and "abandon her policy of

6. *XHNA*, April 18, 1979. See also *XHNA*, May 23, June 28, 1979.
7. *BR*, May 4, 1979, p. 10; August 10, 1979, p. 30; November 30, 1979, p. 13.
8. *XHNA*, April 26, May 18, May 22, July 30, 1979; *BR*, May 4, 1979, pp. 10–11; August 10, 1979, p. 25; November 30, 1979, pp. 13–16; December 7, 1979, pp. 16–19.

opposition and hostility to China".[9] In all this, therefore, China clearly displayed an eagerness to let bygones be bygones and to normalize her relations with Vietnam if only Hanoi would mend its ways and change its course.

If the Chinese attitude betrayed an element of paternalism not entirely dissimilar to that found in Vietnam's approach towards Kampuchea in early 1978, Hanoi apparently perceived the Sino-Vietnamese relations and the entire episode of the Chinese invasion in a completely different light, and launched a vehement attack on China's policy towards Vietnam from the very beginning. Describing the Chinese invasion as a "criminal" act and "a calculated and long-prepared war of aggression in the framework of China's big-power expansionist and hegemonistic policy in Vietnam and in Southeast Asia",[10] Phan Hien, Vietnam's chief delegate to the peace talks, asserted at the first meeting that "the Chinese leaders have for a long time now embarked on a course aimed at compelling Vietnam to give up its independent and sovereign policy and to align itself on China".[11] Citing the "border war in the southwest of Vietnam" without actually naming it, the suspension of all Chinese aids at a time of domestic difficulties in Vietnam, the instigation of ethnic Chinese disturbances, as well as the territorial dispute, Hanoi charged that through all these acts Beijing had sought "to encircle and threaten Vietnam from all sides, to resort to a combination of making pressure from the outside with fomenting troubles from the inside, in an attempt to weaken Vietnam and drag it into China's orbit".[12] And it was only after all these attempts had failed that China decided to subjugate Vietnam through the use of force.[13]

---

9. *XHNA*, April 26, May 18, June 28, August 14, 1979.
10. *VNA*, April 18, 1979. See also, *VNA*, April 26, June 28, 1979.
11. *Ibid.*, April 18, 1979.
12. *Ibid.*
13. *Ibid.* Also, *VNA*, April 26, July 5, 1979.

In fact, as the peace talks proceeded, Vietnam became more and more bitter in her verbal attacks on China. By mid-May, Hanoi already charged that China had long harboured hegemonistic and expansionistic designs towards all the three Indochinese nations,[14] and sought to "seize Indochina from the hands of the French and use the three Indochinese peoples to form a front against the revolution and the Soviet Union".[15] Accusing Beijing of "following the path of former Chinese emperors", i.e., the path of "enslaving other peoples", and placing China at the end of a long line of foreign aggressors "intent on splitting the three countries, pitting one against another so as to ultimately dominate all of them", Hanoi claimed that China had "unceasingly sought to foment trouble and conduct subversion" in Laos, and had "long planned to turn Kampuchea into an important military base, an effective springboard for the annexation of the other countries on the Indochinese peninsula and for expansion into Southeast Asia".[16] In the case of Vietnam, China "throughout the past thirty years" had "persistently pursued a policy to keep Vietnam partitioned, weak and dependent on China so as to facilitate its annexation".[17] To support its argument, Hanoi enumerated how China had compromised with the French in the 1950s, how she had sacrificed the Kampuchean communists and detached Laos from Vietnam at Geneva, how she had secretly fostered the Pol Pot group in the 1960s as a "shock force to further her policy", and how she had colluded with U.S. imperialism against the entire socialist bloc and instigated the Pol Pot regime to launch an aggressive war against Vietnam in the 1970s.[18] Moreover, not only had China been half-hearted

---

14. *RH*, May 17, 1979; *VNA*, July 5, 1979.
15. *RH*, May 17, 1979; *VNA*, July 5, 1979.
16. *VNA*, April 26, May 17, July 5, July 18, 1979.
17. *Ibid.*, July 5, 18, 1979.
18. *RH*, May 17, August 18, 1979. *VNA*, April 26, July 5, July 20, 1979.

in assisting Vietnam during the revolutionary war years, but all the aids provided by China in the past thirty years had been also designed to "buy over and pressure Vietnam into their orbit".[19] Repeatedly proclaiming its determination to preserve "its line of independence and sovereignty", Hanoi held that "it was the Chinese rulers and nobody else" who had undermined the traditional friendship between the two countries by creating tension in the region and by invading and threatening Vietnam.[20] Vietnam therefore insisted that the only way of normalizing relations between the two countries was for China to put a permanent end to her aggression in Indochina and to respect Vietnam's independence and sovereignty.[21]

In view of the above fundamental schism in the two countries' perceptions of each other, it is no wonder that the peace talks that began in April had little chance of success from the very outset. In fact, no sooner had the negotiations started than a basic dispute emerged concerning the very purpose and scope of such peace talks. Being the apparent victim of Chinese invasion and still under the threat of renewed attack, Vietnam considered the problem of Chinese aggression as the only substantive issue to be discussed and insisted that the negotiation should be confined strictly to matters immediately related to the restoration of peace and stability in the border region. Thus, at the first meeting Vietnam made a three-point proposal which called for, among others: (1) the cessation of all acts of hostilities and provocation and the withdrawal of all armed forces of both sides to a distance of three to five kilometres from the border; (2) the establishment of a demilitarized zone to be supervised by a joint commission of the two countries; (3) the restoration of normal relations on the basis of respect for independence, sovereignty, territorial integrity, non-aggression,

---

19. *VNA*, July 5, August 1, 9, 14, 1979.
20. *Ibid.*, April 18, April 26, May 18, June 28, July 5, August 14, August 29, September 20, 1979.
21. *Ibid.*, April 18, July 5, July 18, 1979.

non-use of force, and non-interference in the internal affairs of each other.[22] Nowhere in the proposal or the accompanying remarks did Vietnam touch upon Kampuchea or other broader issues at all.[23]

China apparently viewed the negotiation in quite a different light. Having run great risks in launching the military operation and also having sustained considerable losses, Beijing somehow expected Vietnam to have at least learned a lesson from the border war and therefore sought an overall solution to all the issues of conflict between the two countries. Thus, in countering the three-point proposal made by Hanoi, Beijing at the second meeting made an ambitious eight-point proposal covering Kampuchea as well as the ethnic Chinese and territorial disputes. However, the focus of China's attention was clearly on Kampuchea and Vietnam's regional ambitions, which was also the only major subject not discussed in the three previous rounds of high-level negotiations held in 1977 and 1978. In this respect, China proposed essentially three related courses of action for the restoration of normal relations between the two countries. They were: (1) neither side should seek hegemony in Indochina, Southeast Asia or any other part of the world; (2) neither side should station troops in other countries, and those already stationed abroad must be withdrawn to their own country; and (3) neither side should join any military blocs directed against the other, provide military bases to other countries, or use the territories and bases of other countries to threaten, subvert or commit armed aggression against the other side or against any other countries.[24]

As it soon turned out, these two divergent views and starting points also constituted the two "key issues" to which each side

---

22. *Ibid.*, April 18, 1979.
23. *Ibid.* Radio Hanoi did brush aside the Kampuchean issue as entirely outside the scope of the peace talks without making any elaboration. *ST*, April 29, 1979, p. 3.
24. *BR*, May 4, 1979, p. 16.

adamantly insisted on giving priority in the agenda. Hanoi contended that the tension between China and Vietnam had resulted mainly from China's war of aggression and threat of further use of force against Vietnam. Therefore, it was "imperative first and foremost that the two sides should discuss and agree upon urgent measures to secure peace and stability in the border areas of the two countries".[25] If China was really sincere in settling her disputes with Vietnam through negotiations, she should first pay attention to the problems along the Sino-Vietnamese land border and agree to refrain from concentrating troops close to the border and to stop all forms of hostile activities violating the sovereignty and territorial integrity of the other side.[26] Hanoi thus insisted that the negotiations had no other business than to discuss the prevention of another invasion, and that the most immediate task was to "ease the dangerous situation which might lead to a new outbreak of the war", since only when the risk of war in the border area was eliminated could "adequate conditions for reaching a solution to other problems" be created.[27] In order to accomplish this objective, Hanoi at the third session even proposed a draft agreement to be signed immediately by China and Vietnam, which would require both sides to "refrain from offensive activities, armed provocations, firing from one territory to the other on land, on the sea and in the air, and to refrain from any activity endangering the security of each other".[28]

Indeed, from the Vietnamese perspective, without being first free from the threat of another invasion across the border, there was no point in discussing any other substantive issues, and a commitment by China to the peace along the border was a necessary expression of her sincerity in improving relations with Vietnam. But that was not all. To allow the discussion to

---

25. *VNA*, April 18, 1979.
26. *Ibid.*, April 26, June 28, 1979.
27. *Ibid.*, April 26, 1979. *RH*, June 29, 1979.
28. *RH*, June 29, 1979. *VNA*, July 18, 1979.

include Kampuchea or other larger issues would not only put Vietnam in a bad light and give greater credit to China's military action than politically desirable, but would also concede to China more than the existing balance of forces warranted. By underscoring the aggressive character of the Chinese regime and by concentrating on the specific issue of ensuring peace and tranquillity along the land border, Hanoi therefore expected to shift the blame for the tension in Indochina and the deterioration of Sino-Vietnamese relations to Beijing, and at the same time to avoid the responsibility of accounting for its own conduct in Kampuchea. By manoeuvring China into making a pledge to respect Vietnam's sovereignty and territorial integrity, and particularly not to use force or interfere in the internal affairs of other countries, Hanoi in fact sought not only to remove the danger of further armed intervention against Vietnam but also to keep China safely out of Kampuchea. Such a strategy was certainly essential at a time when Vietnam was still in the process of mopping up remnant Khmer forces, since only after stabilizing the Sino-Vietnamese land border and minimizing the risk of another war with China, could Vietnam expect to hold securely to her gains in Kampuchea and proceed to complete the conquest.

China, on the other hand, considered the border conflict as only a symptom and a result, rather than a cause of the woeful state of Sino-Vietnamese relations which could not really be improved unless and until other larger issues were discussed and resolved. Thus, Beijing repeatedly stressed that the serious deterioration of Sino-Vietnamese relations was in the main the outcome of Vietnam's pursuance of regional hegemonism and the resulting hostility towards China. More specifically, it was Vietnam's ambition to set up an Indochinese federation and her aggression against and occupation of Kampuchea, as well as her long series of anti-China activities, that had led to the confrontation between China and Vietnam.[29] The question of

---

29. *BR*, May 4, 1979, pp. 14–15. See also, *XHNA*, July 5 and 18, 1979.

opposing hegemonism was therefore the "crux of the matter",
the "root cause" and the "fundamental issue" in the Sino-
Vietnamese conflict.[30] In order to normalize the relations
between the two countries, therefore, Vietnam must first
commit herself to the principle of refraining from seeking
hegemony in words and then prove her sincerity in deeds by
stopping her anti-China provocations and withdrawing her
troops from Kampuchea.[31] Without a fundamental change in
Vietnam's policy and intention with regard to both China and
Kampuchea, it would be futile to examine the specific, concrete issues.[32] Indeed, in view of the nature and scope of the
Sino-Vietnamese conflict, nothing short of a comprehensive
review of all the major issues of dispute could be considered
as adequate or useful. And without first identifying and removing the underlying causes of conflict or setting forth the general
principles of improving relations, the negotiations simply could
not be expected to be fruitful.

But that was not all. China's preoccupation with matters of
principles or larger issues was apparently also prompted by
the need to rationalize the large-scale Chinese invasion which,
described by China as "a counter-attack in self-defence",
could not be fully justified by either Vietnam's territorial encroachments or the refugee influx or both. And only by
proceeding from the general principle to concrete issues could
Beijing in the peace talks bring up the subject of Kampuchea,
which had not been related explicitly to the border war.
Presumably China calculated that, once Vietnam could be
brought to accept at least the principle of opposing hegemony,
she would be put on the spot right away and be compelled to
make concessions on the specific issues, particularly on Kampuchea. And by linking the deterioration of Sino-Vietnamese
relations to the general situation in Indochina, China also ex-

---

30. *BR*, May 4, 1979, p. 18; *XHNA*, May 18, 23, July 18, 1979.
31. *XHNA*, May 18, 1979.
32. *Ibid.*; *XHNA*, April 30, 1979. Also, *BR*, May 4, 1979, p. 18.

pected to lend the Pol Pot regime the badly needed political support and therefore hopefully slow down the process of Vietnamese conquest. To allow herself to be bogged down in the negotiation by the trivial territorial or border matters would be not only to give credence to Vietnamese charges of Chinese aggression but also to fall into the trap of Vietnam's delaying tactics,[33] thereby allowing the latter to consolidate her control in Kampuchea. And without first being assured that Vietnam would indeed change her policy towards both China and Kampuchea, Beijing certainly did not want to have its own hands tied by promising not to use force again, particularly along the Sino-Vietnamese border which was the only area where China could exert effective pressure upon Vietnam.

However, in the continuing war of words, the respective objectives of the two antagonists regarding Kampuchea or their real motivations in confronting each other also became increasingly clear. Thus, at the third meeting held in May, China already expressed openly her concern about Soviet involvement in Vietnam's ambitions in Southeast Asia. Beijing contended that "the important reason" why Vietnam had been pursuing a policy of opposition and hostility to China was that her "expansionism and hegemonism" was "supported and instigated" by the Soviet Union.[34] In fact, it was the Soviet backing and encouragement that had enabled Vietnam to behave in such an "unbridled" manner against both Kampuchea and China.[35] Moreover, as Beijing viewed it, Vietnam's attempt to form an Indochina federation was "an important part of the Soviet [Union's] social-imperialist policy of a southward drive and its

---

33. After the first round of talks was completed in May, Vietnam's chief negotiator, Phan Hien, said openly that Vietnam was prepared to negotiate with China for five years or even longer, and that she had plenty of time and vice-ministers to do the job. Reported by *Agence France Presse*, Hanoi, May 31, 1979.
34. *BR*, May 11, 1979, p. 19.
35. *Ibid.*, p. 21.

scheme of rigging up an 'Asian Collective Security System' '',
the purpose of which was to "commit aggression and expansion
in Southeast Asia".[36] China's firm support for Kampuchea,
therefore, was precisely to counter the aggressive designs of both
"the big and the small hegemonists" in the region.[37] In early
July, Han Nianlong in fact declared that it was not only
Vietnam's pursuance of regional hegemonism, but also her
"playing the role of an accomplice of the social-imperialists",
that had brought about the current tension between China and
Vietnam and caused the turmoil and wars in Southeast Asia.[38]
In late July, China finally made public in unmistakable terms
her anxiety about the broader implications of Vietnam's adventure in Kampuchea on China and, therefore, the underlying
rationale of her antagonism towards Vietnam, when she
declared: "In forming the Indochinese federation, the Vietnamese authorities want to set up an anti-China base in the
region adjacent to China's southern boundary, and coordinate
with Soviet social-imperialism's global strategy and policy of a
southward drive for world hegemony so as to serve the needs
of its anti-China plot, threaten China's security and jeopardize China's socialist modernization".[39] China could not
tolerate the materialization of this federation because it was
"directed, in part, at China".[40] Consequently, Beijing argued,
if the question of principle or Kampuchea was bypassed, "the
Sino-Vietnamese negotiations can only serve to cover Vietnamese hegemonism and even meet its needs. Under no
circumstances will the Chinese side agree to this".[41] Indeed,
Vietnam's refusal to discuss Kampuchea or the principle of anti-
hegemonism was believed to constitute in itself an admission

---

36. *Ibid.*, p. 20.
37. *Ibid.*, p. 21.
38. *XHNA*, July 5, 1979.
39. *Ibid.*, July 18, 1979.
40. *Ibid.* Also, *XHNA*, August 14, 1979.
41. *Ibid.*, July 14, 18, 1979.

of the illegality of Vietnamese occupation of Kampuchea.[42] And her insistence on stabilizing the Sino-Vietnamese land border as the central issue was nothing but "a camouflage for tightening her control on Laos and strengthening her war of aggression in Kampuchea, and for her war preparations against China".[43]

On the other hand, when Vietnam did eventually comment directly on the Kampuchean issue in late June, she countered China's charges by arguing that the presence of Vietnamese troops in Laos and Kampuchea was completely justified because it was based upon mutual agreement and was, therefore, a matter of "purely bilateral relations among three sovereign countries".[44] As such, it had "absolutely nothing to do with other countries and totally irrelevant to the Vietnam-China talks". By raising issues not belonging to bilateral relations, China was in fact "claiming the right to discuss the affairs of a third, and even a fourth and fifth country".[45] By insisting on the discussion of anti-hegemonism, China was "creating a precondition for the normalization of Sino-Vietnamese relations" and was "trying to impose its will on Vietnam".[46] In demanding the withdrawal of Vietnamese troops from Kampuchea, China was in fact demanding Vietnam to "give up its correct line of independence, sovereignty, and international solidarity".[47] Moreover, Hanoi now openly proclaimed the militant solidarity of the three Indochinese nations as dictated by history: "It should be pointed out that Vietnam, Laos, and Kampuchea are close and friendly neighbours who have been fighting in unity for nearly half a century against their common

---

42. *Ibid.*, June 28, 1979.
43. *Ibid.*
44. *VNA*, June 28, July 5, 1979. *RH*, July 16, 1979.
45. *RH*, June 29, 1979; *VNA*, July 5, 18, 1979.
46. *VNA*, May 19, 28, 1979.
47. *ST*, May 5, 1979, p. 1; May 24, 1979, p. 28. *VNA*, June 28, 1979; *RH*, June 29, 1979.

enemies.... For the sake of their respective vital interests and the victory of the respective revolutions, the peoples of Vietnam, Laos and Kampuchea have relied on one another and achieved cooperation and mutual assistance...."[48] Hanoi therefore contended that the Vietnamese presence in Kampuchea was nothing unusual and no more than a manifestation of Vietnam's "genuine feelings of international solidarity" with her neighbours, which had in fact occurred at least twice before. And just as Vietnam had withdrawn on previous occasions when her "international obligations were fulfilled", so would she bring home her troops this time, but only "after the danger of aggression and intervention created by the Chinese rulers' expansionism and hegemonism has been removed, and the independence, sovereignty and security of Vietnam, Laos, and Kampuchea secured".[49] In any case, Vietnam finally revealed her real intention in Kampuchea when she declared: "The situation in Kampuchea is irreversible".[50]

As no agreement could be reached even on the procedure of conducting the negotiations, the peace talks were soon turned into a forum for trading charges and countercharges. By refusing to consider the Vietnamese proposal of adopting urgent measures to ensure peace along the border, China was accused of practising "big-nation hegemonism" and "evading the responsibility for their criminal war of aggression against the Vietnamese people".[51] By dodging the question of hegemonism, Vietnam was also charged with "lacking good faith" and "evading the crucial and substantive issues" in the Sino-Vietnamese conflict.[52] That the negotiations had absolutely no effect upon Vietnam's policy in Kampuchea can be seen in the escalated efforts Hanoi made to consolidate its grip on Kam-

---

48. *VNA*, July 5, 1979.
49. *Ibid.*
50. *Agence France Presse*, Beijing, May 2, 1979; *VNA*, July 18, 1979.
51. *VNA*, May 18, June 28, July 5, 1979.
52. *XHNA*, May 18, June 28, July 5, 1979.

puchea throughout 1979. In fact, on March 22, even before the peace talks started, a Lao-Kampuchean Agreement on Economic, Cultural, Scientific and Technological Cooperation was hastily concluded under the auspices of Hanoi, thereby completing the final official step linking Indochina's three countries in an effective entity. The Agreement not only ensured identical foreign and internal policies of the three countries, but also allowed free flow of manpower and resources across their borders, thereby giving a more definite shape to a *de facto* Indochinese federation.[53] In fact, Western military sources confirmed that by late March, Pathet Lao forces had already entered Kampuchea to participate in the war against the Khmer Rouge.[54] A massive programme of population resettlement was also launched at about the same time in a clear attempt to colonize the more sparsely populated Kampuchea and Laos. By July, Vietnam was reported to have already resettled as many as 200,000 Vietnamese in Kampuchea, mostly in the area east of the Mekong River, as well as "thousands" in southern Laos.[55] This was in addition to the 200,000 Vietnamese troops stationed in Kampuchea and more than 6,000 advisors already in Laos. By August, practically every province of Kampuchea had been placed under the charge of a Vietnamese province through a special "sister province" arrangement.[56] By November, there were reportedly at least 250,000 Vietnamese settled in Kampuchea.[57]

In close coordination with the colonization project was a massive purge of Kampucheans of Chinese descent similar to

53. *Vietnam Courier* (Hanoi), April 1979, p. 11. *Sapordamean Kampuchea* (Kampuchean News Agency) (Phnom Penh), March 23, 1979.
54. *ST*, March 26, 1979, p. 5.
55. *ST*, July 2, 1979, p. 2; August 16, 1979, p. 30. *Bangkok Post*, July 17, 1979, p. 1.
56. *FEER*, August 13, 1979, pp. 17–20; *BR*, November 9, 1979, p. 26.
57. *ST*, November 5, 1979, p. 32.

the persecution of Chinese in Vietnam. The campaign was under way as early as April 1979, and the resulting exodus of ethnic Chinese reached a new peak in late May of 1979, when more than 40,000 Kampucheans of Chinese extraction fled to Thailand in one single week, with another 20,000 pushed by the Vietnamese forces to the Thai border and poised to cross over.[58] In fact, according to Thai military sources, "most Kampucheans fleeing to Thailand are of Chinese descent, and many have been sent to the Thai border aboard Vietnamese trucks".[59] In the meantime, there were recurrent reports that the Vietnamese forces in Kampuchea were systematically starving to death many Kampucheans by diverting large amounts of precious international aid supplies destined for the people into the hands of the Vietnamese troops,[60] by actually preventing the Kampuchean peasants from harvesting their grain,[61] and by even spraying poisonous gas from aircraft against civilians as well as suspected guerrilla strongholds.[62] Kampuchea was being dismembered as a functioning society with dire consequences on the entire Khmer race.

On the battlefield, Hanoi also went all out to intensify its offensive against the retreating Khmer Rouge forces, in an attempt to wipe out Khmer resistance at one final stroke. This was evidenced not only by the continuing increase of Vietnamese troops in Kampuchea from the initial 100,000 to 150,000 by May 1979, and to 200,000 by October 1979,[63] but also by the large-scale military re-supply operation the Soviet Union launched in the spring of 1979 to aid Vietnam in her war ef-

---

58. *ST*, May 23, 1979, p. 1.
59. *ST*, June 6, 1979, p. 2.
60. *The New York Times*, August 9, 1979, p. 3; September 27, 1979, p. 19; October 1, 1979, p. 10; December 3, 1979, p. 11; December 12, 1979, p. 11.
61. *ST*, November 30, 1979, p. 1; December 22, 1979, p. 3.
62. *Voice of Democratic Kampuchea*, September 16, 1979; *The New York Times*, February 18, 1980, p. 8.
63. *ST*, May 5, 1979, p. 1; October 8, 1979, p. 4.

forts, with a total of 79 flights over Thai air space in the short span of two months from April to May alone.[64] In fact, by late April, only one week after the peace talks had started, the Vietnamese forces in a massive, two-pronged operation had already cornered an estimated 60,000 Khmer forces in western Kampuchea, and Vietnamese units were beginning to cross into Thai territory in hot pursuit of the Kampuchean forces.[65] To intimidate Thailand into adopting a strictly neutral policy, the Heng Samrin regime even warned Thailand of "dangerous consequences" for allowing China to smuggle arms to the Khmers through Thai territory.[66] By November 1979, Hanoi had already massed 40,000 troops along the Thai-Kampuchean border in preparation for a major dry-season offensive to wipe out the Khmer forces.[67]

In the process of executing her anticipated final assault on the Khmer Rouge and consolidating her control over Kampuchea and Laos, Vietnam also did not take any chances along her northern frontier. Immediately after the war, large units of crack regular troops together with large amounts of war materials, including some of the most sophisticated weapons supplied by the Soviet Union, were transported to the Sino-Vietnamese border areas.[68] In fact, the northern provinces were quickly turned into a gigantic military base.[69] In beefing up its defence installations and buttressing its defence posture, Hanoi not only relied upon the Russians for technical and logistic support but also deliberately drew even closer to Moscow, by inviting more Soviet technical and military advisors into

64. *ST*, May 25, 1979, p. 1.
65. *ST*, April 23, 1979, p. 1; May 4, 1979, p. 3.
66. *Sapordamean Kampuchea*, February 27, 1979; *Radio Bangkok*, March 1, 2, 1979. Also, *ST*, March 5, 1979, p. 1; *MD*, October 14, 1979, p. 14.
67. *ST*, November 15, 1979, p. 40.
68. *The New York Times*, March 16, 1979, p. 1; *ST*, March 17, 1979, p. 3; March 27, 1979, p. 28; October 8, 1979, p. 4.
69. *ST*, May 4, 1979, p. 1.

Vietnam and by opening up Vietnamese air bases and seaports to Soviet use.[70] By May there were reportedly already 7,000 Soviet, Cuban, and East German advisers in Indochina.[71] Advanced Soviet military aircraft and naval vessels, including the long-range TU-95 bombers and nuclear attack submarines, had also begun to make visits to Vietnam.[72] The purpose was clearly to deter another Chinese invasion. By August, Vietnam was confident enough of making more progress in Kampuchea and of the support from the Soviet Union to proclaim once again the "unshakable military solidarity and friendship" between the three Indochinese peoples and to reiterate the "irreversible" nature of the Kampuchean situation.[73] In particular, Hanoi warned Beijing that China should "think it over" before embarking upon another war against Vietnam, and declared that it "would not be taken by surprise this time".[74] To buttress its position further, Hanoi in fact went as far as to declare openly its reliance on "the military solidarity, friendship and cooperation between Vietnam and the Soviet Union as a *firm guarantee* for their victory in the socialist construction and national defence".[75]

China, on the other hand, was also determined that the lesson she had intended to teach Vietnam was indeed learned. In fact, the fall of Phnom Penh to Vietnamese forces did not lead to the slightest change in China's position on Kampuchea. On January 9, only two days after Vietnam had captured Phnom Penh, Deng Xiaoping told visiting U.S. senators that China would continue to support the Pol Pot regime and did not consider the fall of Phnom Penh as the end of the

---

70. *ST*, March 30, 1979, p. 36; April 13, 1979, p. 3.
71. *ST*, May 3, 1979, p. 1.
72. *ST*, May 3, 1979, p. 1; May 12, 1979, p. 6.
73. *Vietnam Courier*, September 1979, p. 2. Also, *VNA*, August 22, 26, 1979.
74. *ST*, August 8, 1979, p. 3; August 13, 1979, p. 5.
75. *ST*, October 2, 1979, p. 28.

struggle.[76] A week later, Hua Guofeng told visiting Thai Deputy Premier Sunthorn Hongladarom that China would support Kampuchea "through to the end" against Vietnamese aggression.[77] A Chinese governmental statement issued on January 14 formally pledged that China "will, as always, firmly stand by the Kampuchean people and do her utmost to support and aid the Kampuchean people in every way".[78] By late January, Beijing was already busily resupplying the Khmer Rouge through Thai territory and using Chinese ships.[79] In early April, when the fighting had begun to spill over into Thai territory, the Chinese ambassador to Thailand, Zhang Weilih, while reiterating China's determination to give "all the assistance necessary" to the Pol Pot regime, told the *Bangkok Post* that China would help Thailand if she should be attacked.[80] In late June, apparently to counter Vietnam's warning to Thailand not to help the Khmers, Deng Xiaoping reassured Thailand that China would help Thailand "in every way" if she should be invaded by Vietnam, and even declared: "Any threat to Thailand is a threat to China".[81] In view of the fact that the Khmer Rouge had recently used Thai territory as an escape route and received their major supplies through Thai territory, the repeated Chinese warnings against Vietnamese encroachments on Thai territory were clearly aimed at deterring any massive Vietnamese incursions into Thailand which would jeopardize the very survival of the Khmer Rouge forces.

To make sure that the Khmer Rouge could withstand the Vietnamese onslaught, China throughout 1979 also kept alive her threat to use force against Vietnam again. Thus, in announ-

---

76. *XHNA*, January 9, 1979. Also, *BR*, January 12, 1979, p. 2.
77. *Renmin Ribao*, January 14, 1979, p. 1.
78. *BR*, January 19, 1979, p. 3.
79. *ST*, February 1, 1979, p. 2; February 8, 1979, p. 3; February 11, 1979, p. 2.
80. *ST*, April 2, 1979, p. 28.
81. *ST*, June 27, 1979, p. 30.

cing the withdrawal of Chinese troops from Vietnam in early March, Beijing declared that China would counterattack again if Vietnam renewed armed provocations.[82] In early May, at a time when the Vietnamese forces were bottling up retreating Khmer forces in western Kampuchea, Deng Xiaoping told visiting UN Secretary-General, Dr. Waldheim, that China "reserves the right to act and will teach Vietnam another lesson".[83] In July, Li Xiannian repeated China's warning when he told the *Newsweek* magazine in an interview: "China does not rule out the possibility of another strike against Vietnam".[84] The same warning was reiterated many times in the second half of 1979 by other high-ranking Chinese officials, including Premier Hua Guofeng.[85]

In order to demonstrate that China meant business, Beijing not only continued to station over twelve divisions of troops close to the Sino-Vietnamese border, with five army corps behind them, but also carried out a series of manoeuvres designed to tie down a substantial number of Vietnamese units along the border, and to deter Vietnam from any further massive and sustained offensives against the Khmer Rouge forces.[86] Thus, in late July, Beijing declared four "danger" zones in the air space covering part of the Gulf of Tonkin and areas west of the Paracels Islands, apparently in preparation for escalated air activity in the region.[87] In the meantime, a large number of photographs showing Chinese missiles and troops in training manoeuvres were released amidst reports that China's 42nd army stationed near Hong Kong was being moved to the

---

82. *XHNA*, March 5, 1979.
83. *ST*, May 3, 1979, p. 1.
84. *Newsweek*, July 16, 1979, p. 59.
85. *ST*, July 27, 1979, p. 1; October 8, 1979, p. 1; October 26, 1979, p. 1. *The New York Times*, December 8, 1979, p. 3.
86. *ST*, May 4, 1979, p. 1; May 10, 1979, p. 1; August 15, 1979, p. 38. *The New York Times*, December 20, 1979, p. 5.
87. *XHNA*, July 23, 1979.

Vietnamese border.[88] In October, in anticipation of a new Vietnamese dry-season offensive, Beijing went one step further to increase its aerial bombing practices on its side of the Sino-Vietnamese border, and Western sources once again reported abnormal movements and reinforcements of Chinese troops which were similar to those detected immediately prior to the 1979 war, thereby giving the impression that China might indeed teach Vietnam another lesson soon.[89] In fact, Beijing somewhat deliberately suggested to visiting American Vice-President Mondale in early October that the second lesson might have to be administered to Vietnam around November when the drive against the Pol Pot forces would have gathered steam.[90]

In addition to all this rattling of sabres, China also seemed to have made it a policy after the 1979 war to respond to every single Vietnamese armed provocation or incursion into Chinese territory with determined counter-attacks, and to conduct what Hanoi branded as "psychological warfare" along the entire border, if only to exert continuing pressure on Vietnam and to tie down Vietnamese forces. As a result, the armed clashes along the border became once again a frequent phenomenon, particularly from July on, with each side enumerating in great detail the nature and scope of such incidents.[91] In late November, Hanoi in fact charged that China had committed over 1,000 armed provocations in violation of Vietnamese territory during the six-month period following the end of the border war, whereas Beijing also accused Vietnam of making

---

88. See *Renmin Ribao*, July 23, 28, 30, August 1, 1979; *ST*, August 13, 1979, p. 5.
89. *ST*, October 26, 1979, p. 1; October 31, 1979, p. 2.
90. *ST*, October 8, 1979, p. 14.
91. For instance, *XHNA*, July 4, August 5, September 3, October 6, November 20, December 3, 1979. For Vietnamese charges, see for instance, *VNA*, July 10, August 27, September 6, 29, November 1, December 5, 1979.

more than 370 military incursions into China's border regions during the three months of August to October alone.[92] And the tense situation persisted into early 1980 with no sign of relaxation.[93] As a military solution to the Kampuchean conflict had remained Vietnam's chosen path, and as China was determined to meet the Vietnamese challenge in the battlefield, the futility of carrying on the peace negotiations also became increasingly clear. Thus, on February 7, 1980, Beijing refused to resume the stalled peace talks, charging that Vietnam had used the talks as "a cover for her aggression against Kampuchea, threats to Thailand, and armed provocations against China", thereby virtually suspending the negotiations which had lasted for nearly a year.[94] The peace talks were formally called off by Beijing on March 6, 1980.[95]

---

92. *XHNA*, November 20, 1979; *VNA*, November 24, 1979.
93. China claimed that there were more than 200 armed incidents in January 1980 alone. *XHNA*, February 7, 1980.
94. *Ibid.*
95. *XHNA*, March 6, 1980.

6
Beijing's Diplomacy

By virtue of its broad implications, the Sino-Vietnamese conflict over Kampuchea is not confined to the Indochinese peninsula but has also been waged at a higher plane of international diplomacy since 1979, when both countries launched an intensive campaign to rally global and regional support for their policies. Having attempted to change Vietnam's policy towards Kampuchea, first by persuasion and then by force, and yet unable to achieve her aim, China in the spring of 1979 quickly threw in her weight behind the growing international opposition to the Vietnamese occupation of Kampuchea, and began to play a major role in boosting and sustaining such political pressure on Vietnam. In doing so, Beijing apparently expected to win, at a crucial stage of the Kampuchean war, the additional, valuable moral and political support for the Khmer Rouge which China could only assist in a limited material way, and therefore to forestall any attempt made by Hanoi and its allies to legitimize the Vietnamese conquest. In order to attain these objectives, China adopted an essentially legalistic approach towards the Kampuchean issue and capitalized on its international implications. Thus, beginning with the emergency UN Security Council meeting in March 1979, Beijing in all international forums or debates on Kampuchea repeatedly stressed that the Vietnamese occupation of Kampuchea was an act of "naked aggression" across international boundaries and a "colonial war in which the strong bullies the weak with the aim of subjugating a small independent nation".[1] As such, it

---

1. *BR*, March 23, 1979, pp. 26–27; October 12, 1979, p. 15; November 23, 1979, p. 22.

had "trampled underfoot the UN Charter and fundamental principles of international law" and must not be condoned.[2] For this reason, the UN also had "an unshirkable responsibility" to take effective measures to resolve the Kampuchean issue.[3] Moreover, since the Heng Samrin regime in Kampuchea was no more than a "puppet" created "at bayonet point" by the Vietnamese army, it should be denied the right of representation at all international bodies.[4] In this connection, Beijing took pains to remind the international community repeatedly that recognition of a government did not mean approval of its policies, and that continuing recognition of Democratic Kampuchea was "a matter of principle", as it upheld the sovereignty and independence of a member of the United Nations.[5] To do otherwise would be to acknowledge that military aggression and interference with another country's internal affairs was permissible, a situation which could only throw the international community into chaos.[6]

But that was not all. Beijing contended that Vietnam's occupation of Kampuchea and her domination of Laos was not an "isolated event" or "local issue", since it not only revealed Hanoi's ambition to dominate the entire Indochina but also represented "an important component of [the] Soviet [Union's] attempt to further its strategy of seeking world hegemony".[7] More specifically, Vietnam had invited the Soviets in because she needed Moscow's support in realizing her regional ambi-

---

2. *Ibid.*, March 23, 1979, p. 27; August 31, 1979, p. 25; October 12, 1979, p. 15; November 23, 1979, p. 22.
3. *Ibid.*, March 23, 1979, p. 27; October 12, 1979, p. 17.
4. *XHNA*, October 9, 1979; May 10, 1980; Also, *BR*, October 12, 1979, p. 15; September 8, 1980, p. 11.
5. *BR*, September 28, 1979, p. 26; September 8, 1980, p. 11.
6. *Ibid.*, September 28, 1979, p. 26; October 26, 1979, p. 11; September 8, 1980, p. 11; October 6, 1980, p. 11.
7. *Ibid.*, March 23, 1979, p. 27; October 12, 1979, pp. 15–16; October 26, 1979, p. 11; November 23, 1979, p. 22; October 6, 1980, pp. 12–23.

tions. And Moscow had backed Hanoi because it needed Vietnam in order to "push its policy of driving south, [and] link up its strategic deployments in the Pacific and the Indian Ocean".[8] In fact, with the growing presence of the Soviet navy and air force in Vietnam and Kampuchea, Indochina had already become "a forward base for Soviet southward expansion."[9] Therefore, the Kampuchean problem, China argued, was a manifestation, not so much of the conflict between China and Vietnam or between the Indochinese and other Southeast Asian states, as of the Soviet and Vietnamese threat to the entire region. As such, it was of "global significance" and required common efforts and united action of all "justice-upholding" countries in order to counter this threat.[10] By the same token, in lending a hand to Kampuchea, Beijing was not merely abiding by its consistent policy of supporting the "just struggle of the Indochinese states to win and safeguard national independence", but was also containing the Soviet drive towards global hegemony.[11] And Beijing warned that, unless Vietnam's armed aggression was checked in time and Hanoi condemned by the world organization in the strongest possible terms, greater peril would befall the whole of Southeast Asia and there would be more wars in the world.[12]

Whereas China's interpretation of the Kampuchean situation was not necessarily shared by the overwhelming majority of the members of the international community, it did reveal her traditional perception of Kampuchea and her new anxiety about Soviet encirclement of China from Southeast Asia. It was also the best strategy Beijing could have adopted in order to ensure

---

8. *Ibid.*, October 12, 1979, p. 15; November 23, 1979, p. 22.
9. *Ibid.*, October 6, 1979, p. 12; August 25, 1980, pp. 10–11. Also, *XHNA*, August 4, 1979; September 20, 1980.
10. *BR*, October 12, 1979, pp. 16–17; October 26, 1979, p. 11. *XHNA*, September 3 and October 15, 1980.
11. *BR*, October 12, 1979, p. 17; *XHNA*, September 15 and 17, 1980.
12. *BR*, October 12, 1979, p. 17; November 23, 1979, p. 22.

maximum gains. In view of the bad name the notorious Pol Pot regime had established for itself during the three-year reign of terror from 1975 to 1978, only by adhering to the legalistic principles could China expect to muster credible international sympathy for the ousted Khmer government and at the same time justify her own support for it. In internationalizing the Kampuchean issue and insisting on a role of the United Nations in the Kampuchean conflict, China apparently sought to generate a degree of pressure on Vietnam which she herself was unable to exert, by putting Hanoi on the spot and therefore forcing it to account for its conduct in Kampuchea. Moreover, since China had the disadvantage of representing the bigger power in the Sino-Vietnamese conflict, only by capitalizing on the broader implications of the Kampuchean war and the Soviet role in the Vietnamese adventure could Beijing expect to convince the international community of the urgent and serious nature of the Kampuchean crisis and the righteousness of China's continuing intervention in the whole affair.

In order to check effectively the "Soviet-Vietnamese expansion" in the Southeast Asian region, therefore, China from the very beginning adopted a hard-line stance on Vietnam's occupation of Kampuchea and pledged her full support for all proposals or formulas that called for an immediate and complete withdrawal of Vietnamese troops from Kampuchea, and considered this as the "key" to the solution of the Kampuchean question.[13] Beijing in fact insisted that a complete Vietnamese withdrawal was the prerequisite for any political settlement of the Kampuchean problem.[14] As Huang Hua put it in October 1979, while China was not opposed to a political solution as such, "the condition will have to be created for it", and as long as Vietnam refused to withdraw her troops, the only effective

---

13. *Ibid.*, March 23, 1979, pp. 26–27; August 31, 1979, p. 25; October 12, 1979, p. 17; October 6, 1980, p. 14.
14. *Ibid.*, October 12, 1979, p 17; October 6, 1980, p. 14. *XHNA*, May 10, 1980; July 12, 1981.

course of action was to support the resistance forces and intensify the fighting, and to increase diplomatic and economic pressures so as to "saddle Hanoi with increasing burdens and difficulties" until Hanoi felt the need for compromise.[15] Therefore, while actively supporting an international framework for the settlement of the Kampuchean question, Beijing was against holding any special international conference on Kampuchea, unless the withdrawal of Vietnamese troops was made the primary purpose of such a conference and meticulously executed within a time limit. And to test Vietnam's sincerity as well as to ensure that such a meeting would not create an atmosphere of appeasement, Beijing throughout 1979 and 1980 even deemed it necessary for Vietnam at least to begin the troop withdrawal before such a conference was convened.[16]

China's uncompromising stance on Vietnam was apparently based upon a realistic calculation of the existing balance of forces in Kampuchea. Indeed, in view of the glaring disparity between the Vietnamese occupation forces and the Khmer Rouge, it was almost impossible to reverse the tide of war in Kampuchea without a prior Vietnamese withdrawal. And any concession made to the status quo in Kampuchea could only imply acquiescence in the fait accompli of the Vietnamese occupation. But that was not all. Being the principal supporter of the Khmer Rouge and in fact the only country which was both willing and powerful enough to sustain the anti-Vietnamese struggle, China could not have expressed her determination to thwart Vietnam's plans in Kampuchea or lend effective moral support to the resistance forces by demanding anything less than a complete Vietnamese pull-out from Kampuchea or wavering on the question of continuing armed struggle. Having had the

---

15. *BR*, October 26, 1979, p. 11. Also, *BR*, March 24, 1980, pp. 6–7; January 12, 1981, p. 3. *XHNA*, July 11–12, 1981. *ST*, March 18, 1980, p. 32; March 20, 1980, p. 9. *FEER*, July 17, 1981, p. 13.
16. *BR*, September 22, 1980, pp. 3–4; January 12, 1981, p. 3. *XHNA*, July 11, 1981; *FEER*, July 17, 1981, pp. 13–14.

unpleasant experience of conducting four separate rounds of high-level but futile negotiations with Vietnam in the course of two years on all the major issues of bilateral conflict,[17] China also had good reasons to believe that, short of a voluntary but complete Vietnamese withdrawal from Kampuchea, a political settlement guaranteeing an independent Kampuchea could not be negotiated in the conference hall but had to be won on the battlefield.

China's insistence on building up maximum pressures upon Vietnam and on continuing the war in Kampuchea was such that not only did she keep alive her threat of teaching Vietnam a second lesson throughout 1979,[18] but also she took pains to assure repeatedly the ASEAN countries in general and Thailand in particular of her readiness to lend effective support to them in case of the widening of the armed conflict in Indochina. Thus, Deng Xiaoping as early as June 1979 told Thai Air Marshal Dawee that China would help Thailand "in every way" if she was invaded by Vietnam.[19] The assurance was repeated in October 1979 when Deng again declared to Thailand's Air Chief, Marshal Harin Hongskula: "China will stand on the side of the ASEAN countries if Vietnam attacks them. It will stand on the side of Thailand if Vietnam attacks it".[20] In late November, when Vietnam had launched a dry-season offensive against the Khmer forces in western Kampuchea, Beijing went as far as promising all ASEAN countries "all possible support, including military assistance", if any one of them was

---

17. See my articles "The Sino-Vietnamese Territorial Dispute", *Asia-Pacific Community*, Spring 1980, pp. 130–65; and "The Sino-Vietnamese Dispute over the Ethnic Chinese", *The China Quarterly*, June 1982, pp. 195–230.

18. *ST*, May 3, 1979, p. 1; July 10, 1979, p. 26; July 27, 1979, p. 1; October 8, 1979, p. 1; October 26, 1979, p. 1.

19. *Ibid.*, June 27, 1979, p. 30.

20. *BR*, November 2, 1979, p. 3.

attacked.[21] In early December, a Chinese military delegation led by Deputy Chief of the PLA was sent to Thailand in a gesture of China's solidarity with Thailand, as well as to review the border situation.[22] This was followed in late December by another statement of Deng Xiaoping which explicitly declared: "China would take action if Vietnam sends troops into Thai territory".[23]

However, Beijing's intensive involvement in the Kampuchean war and its enthusiasm in propping up the notorious Khmer Rouge inevitably had the effect of heightening the long-standing suspicions the ASEAN states harboured of China's objectives in the region, thereby keeping them somewhat aloof from the entire conflict. Beijing was apparently aware of this, as well as the notoriety of the Khmer Rouge. Hence, one of the initial diplomatic efforts China made after the fall of Phnom Penh was to encourage the Khmer Rouge to broaden its base of support by forming alliances with other anti-Vietnamese groups. The establishment of such a broadly based alliance was considered as essential not only to improving the international image of the Khmer Rouge, thereby augmenting its legitimacy, but also in ensuring the viability of the entire resistance movement. Thus, as early as February 1979, China called for a broad united front and described it as "a magic weapon for victory" in a nationalist struggle against foreign aggression.[24] In early April, the Chinese Ambassador to Thailand, Zhang Weilih, for the first time hinted that China was prepared to support all patriotic Kampuchean resistance groups against

---

21. *ST*, November 22, 1979, p. 8; November 23, 1979, p. 1; November 24, 1979, p. 4
22. *XHNA*, November 30 and December 8, 1979.
23. *ST*, December 20, 1979, p. 3. Similar assurances were made also throughout 1980. See *BR*, February 18, 1980, p. 7; July 7, 1980, p. 7; August 11, 1980, p. 7. *XHNA*, April 22, 1980. *FEER*, August 8, 1980, p. 9.
24. *BR*, February 16, 1979, p. 23.

Vietnamese aggression.[25] It was also clearly at China's urging that in early September of 1979, on the eve of the UN General Assembly debate on Kampuchea, the Khmer Rouge took the initiative of making public a new political programme drafted for the specific purpose of "uniting in a large national front all the patriotic and democratic forces, at home and abroad", in order to fight the Vietnamese. The programme was to replace the 1976 socialist constitution as the "provisional basic decree" and therefore to pave the way for cooperation between all anti-Vietnamese forces.[26] While it received the immediate endorsement of China, Deng Xiaoping in late October already openly promised to "use every appropriate means" to support "all patriotic Kampuchean forces".[27] The formal adoption of the programme in December in fact led to a reshuffle of the Democratic Kampuchean government, with Khieu Samphan replacing the notorious Pol Pot as Prime Minister. In a message sent to Prince Sihanouk in September and again in December, Khieu Samphan actually requested the former Kampuchean ruler to assume the chairmanship of the newly formed Kampuchean Patriotic and Democratic Front of Great Nation, and to resume his former position as Head of State.[28]

However, skepticism from the ASEAN states about the Khmer Rouge's mandate was such that a united front under its actual leadership could arouse little interest among them. In order to make the conflict in Kampuchea not appear one exclusively between China and Vietnam, and to win the ASEAN countries definitely over to the side of the resistance movement, Beijing in early 1980 apparently decided to seek closer policy coordination with these countries and to accommodate their

---

25. *ST*, April 2, 1979, p. 28.
26. *BR*, September 14, 1979, pp. 19–20.
27. *Ibid.*, November 2, 1979, p. 3.
28. *XHNA*, September 6, 1979; *Voice of Democratic Kampuchea*, December 26, 1979; *BR*, January 7, 1980, p. 9; *ST*, December 21, 1979, p. 1.

views as much as possible. Thus, Chinese Foreign Minister Huang Hua was sent to Southeast Asia in March and again in May of 1980 to sound out the views of the ASEAN countries on the question of a united front. This was followed by visits to China by Thai Prime Minister General Prem in October 1980 and by Singapore Prime Minister Lee Kuan Yew in November of the same year. Apparently as a result of the October and November consultations, a basic agreement was reached on the format and conditions of a coalition government of all anti-Vietnamese resistance forces which would now include the anti-communist Son Sann group, as well as the neutralist Sihanouk group. A division of labour was also arranged whereby China would try to persuade Sihanouk to join the coalition whereas Singapore and Thailand would use their influence on the non-communist Son Sann.[29] During these meetings, China also agreed for the first time that the coalition government was to be non-communist in orientation and led by either Son Sann or Prince Sihanouk rather than by Khieu Samphan. Beijing even promised to help with the growth of the military strength of the non-communist resistance groups.[30]

Moreover, to dispel whatever doubts the ASEAN countries might still have of China's intentions in Indochina, Beijing from late 1980 on also repeatedly affirmed its support not only for a free general election in Kampuchea under UN supervision after the Vietnamese withdrawal but also for an eventually independent, non-aligned Kampuchea.[31] Thus, Chinese leaders told Lee Kuan Yew in November 1980 that China was not seeking a pro-Beijing government in Kampuchea but only one that was independent and neutral.[32] In a further gesture of solidarity with the ASEAN states, China towards the end of

---

29. *ST*, November 12, 1980, p. 1.
30. *Ibid*. See also, *FEER*, February 6, 1981, p. 8; *BR*, February 9, 1981, pp. 14–15.
31. *BR*, October 6, 1980, p.14; *FEER*, August 17, 1981, p. 14.
32. *ST*, November 13, 1980, pp. 1, 34.

1980 decided to drop her condition of at least a partial Vietnamese withdrawal as a prerequisite for the holding of an
international conference on Kampuchea, in order to sustain the
momentum of political pressure on Vietnam.[33] In February
1981, Chinese Premier Zhao Ziyang made a special visit to
Thailand, during which he explicitly stated China's willingness
to join an international guarantee following the Vietnamese
withdrawal that would ensure not only the independence and
sovereignty of Kampuchea, but also the non-use of Kampuchean territory for encroaching upon the sovereignty of other
countries in Southeast Asia.[34] To match her words with deeds,
in early February 1981, China apparently persuaded Sihanuok
to join the united front coalition by promising military aid to
his supporters.[35] In the ensuing negotiations between Khieu
Samphan and Prince Sihanouk in March, the Khmer Rouge
went as far as accepting virtually all the conditions made by
the prince, including the adoption of a multi-party parliamen-
tary system after the Vietnamese withdrawal.[36] In late April,
China in a much publicized move delivered a major arms shipment to Son Sann's forces which included mortars and rockets,
and was enough to equip 3,000 men.[37] This was followed by
Beijing's announcement in early May that China was ready to
arm another 3,000 men for Sihanouk's group, on the only condition that the arms would not be used against the Khmer Rouge
or Son Sann forces.[38]

   All these measures, while designed to demonstrate China's
sincerity in supporting the united resistance movement, were
apparently also aimed at mustering maximum support for the
Khmer Rouge in the forthcoming UN-sponsored international

---

33. *Ibid.*, November 24, 1980, p. 2. Also, *BR*, July 20, 1981, p. 16.
34. *BR*, February 9, 1981, pp. 14–15.
35. *ST*, February 9, 1981, p. 2.
36. *Ibid.*, March 13, 1981, p. 3; *BR*, March 23, 1981, p. 10.
37. *BR*, May 1, 1981, p. 1; May 3, 1981, p. 1.
38. *Ibid.*, May 11, 1981, p. 1.

conference on Kampuchea. In fact, throughout the first half of 1981, when the conference was in the final planning stage, Beijing repeatedly declared that China had no intention of seeking hegemony abroad and was opposing not Vietnam as such, but merely her policies of expansionism, and that once the Vietnamese troops were withdrawn from Kampuchea, normal relations between China and Vietnam could be immediately restored.[39] During the UN Conference on Kampuchea held in July 1981, Beijing lent full support to the ASEAN stand that, after the war was over, the Kampuchean people should be allowed to choose the form of government they desired free from outside interference. It also formally proposed a solution of the entire problem which called for a free election in Kampuchea under UN supervision after the Vietnamese withdrawal, and an international guarantee of the independence and neutrality of Kampuchea by all the five permanent Security Council members plus Vietnam and the ASEAN countries.[40]

In a further attempt to convince the ASEAN states of China's clear conscience, as well as to strengthen their united stand against Vietnam, Chinese Premier Zhao Ziyang made a tour of four ASEAN countries in August 1981. Reiterating China's wishes to see only an "independent, neutral, and non-aligned Kampuchea", Zhao explicitly told his ASEAN hosts that China had no intention of imposing a Marxist regime on Kampuchea or making it a satellite state. Nor did China want to create any sphere of influence in Southeast Asia.[41] He also took pains to assure the ASEAN nations that relations between the Chinese Communist Party and the communist parties in Southeast Asia were issues "left over by history" and were no more than "political and moral" in nature. Any problem involving these parties was "a domestic problem of these countries" and China

---

39. *BR*, February 9, 1981, p. 15. Also, *XHNA*, July 11 and 14, 1981.
40. *XHNA*, July 16, 1981; *BR*, July 20, 1981, pp. 14–15.
41. *BR*, August 24, 1981, p. 6. Also, *XHNA*, August 10–13, 1981; *FEER*, August 21, 1981, pp. 11–13.

would "never intervene" in its handling. Nor would China interfere with the internal affairs of these countries.[42]

It was after all these diplomatic efforts that the leaders of the three major forces in the Kampuchean resistance movement were finally brought together in September 1981 in a tripartite conference held in Singapore to discuss the formation of a coalition government in Kampuchea. In February 1982, China responded to Thailand's request by agreeing to host a second round of the tripartite meeting in Beijing, but before the scheduled meeting, the arms requested by Sihanouk were already delivered to his 3,000 supporters inside Kampuchea.[43] Nevertheless, as it turned out, the conference was stillborn since only the Khmer Rouge and Sihanouk's group participated whereas Son Sann chose to stay out — presumably in order not to associate himself too closely with a communist power. After this disappointing experience, Beijing decided to further lower its profile in the entire Kampuchean conflict by confining its own role to that of a follower of ASEAN. Thus, when the talks for the coalition government were deadlocked in the spring of 1982, and when a few ASEAN countries began to show impatience with the Khmer Rouge, China restricted her activity to urging the three resistance groups to place their national interest above all, and merely cautioned the ASEAN countries against any wavering in their support for the resistance cause or in their opposition to Vietnam without, however, making any concrete proposal herself.[44] In fact, Beijing in early March made the hitherto clearest disclaimer of its preference for the Khmer Rouge when Vice Premier Han Nianlong declared that since all the three resistance groups had been China's "old friends", China had no special interest in the Khmer Rouge

---

42. *BR*, August 17, 1981, p. 8; August 24, 1981, pp. 5-6. *FEER*, August 21, 1981, p. 13.
43. *ST*, February 24, 1982, p. 1.
44. *XHNA*, January 16, 30; February 26; March 1, 7, 27; May 10, 11; 1982.

for ideological reasons nor did she want to force any single group to power.[45]

Similarly, when the final agreement was reached in Kuala Lumpur between the three resistance groups on the formal establishment of a coalition government on June 22, Beijing merely reported it as "a major development" and an "important step in uniting all anti-Vietnamese forces" without, however, showing much overt enthusiasm.[46] In fact, while reaffirming her firm support for the anti-Vietnamese movement until its final victory, China declined to confirm or deny openly whether she would step up her military aid to any one of the three component groups of the coalition government, but chose to increase her assistance discreetly.[47] Chinese leaders after the establishment of the coalition government nevertheless continued to repeat China's wishes to see Kampuchea become a neutral, non-aligned country, and pledged to cooperate with ASEAN in resolving the entire problem.[48] Deng Xiaoping in fact told Sihanouk in Beijing in late July: "China's support for the new Democratic Kampuchean government was not a short-term, tactical move. Even after the Kampuchean people's complete victory in the anti-Vietnamese struggle, the three parties will need to cooperate in order to build Kampuchea into a peaceful, neutral, and non-aligned nation".[49]

In a further effort to demonstrate that China had no intention to bleed Vietnam white nor to oppose Vietnam for the sake of opposition, but was quite flexible in her approach to the entire Kampuchean problem, Beijing on March 1, 1983 declared

---

45. *FEER*, March 12, 1982, pp. 12–13. See also *XHNA*, May 11, 1982.

46. *XHNA*, June 24, 1982. *BR*, July 5, 1982, p. 9; July 12, 1982, p. 3.

47. *ST*, June 23, 1982, p. 8; June 24, 1982, p. 1. Sihanouk's group received another major shipment of arms in early May of 1982 without publicity. *Nation Review* (Bangkok), July 9, 1982.

48. *XHNA*, July 17, 20, 22, 1982. *Renmin Ribao*, July 10, 1982.

49. *XHNA*, July 22, 1982.

in a five-point proposal that China would be willing to resume talks with Vietnam for the normalization of relations, if only Hanoi undertook to commit itself openly to a complete withdrawal from Kampuchea and withdraw the first batch of troops. And along with each additional withdrawal of Vietnamese troops from Kampuchea, China promised to take practical steps to improve her relations with Vietnam.[50] On the same occasion, Beijing once again expressed its support for the principle of self-determination for all Kampucheans after the Vietnamese withdrawal was completed, and its wishes to see "an independent, peaceful, neutral, and non-aligned Kampuchea". China also reiterated her willingness to enter into a joint commitment with other interested countries "to refrain from any form of interference in the internal affairs of Kampuchea", once a genuinely free election was held under the supervision of the United Nations.[51] This policy was reiterated by Zhao Ziyang and other Chinese leaders in early August and again in September, and has since remained unchanged.[52]

Clearly, all these efforts were made to ensure the ASEAN countries's continuing support for the Khmer resistance movement which China realized to be indispensable to the sustaining of diplomatic pressure on Vietnam. As such, they were also essential to keeping the Kampuchean issue under international spotlight. In fact, only by working closely with ASEAN as a partner in, not an architect of, the international united front against Vietnam could China expect to isolate Hanoi effectively. Only by pledging to strive towards a neutral and non-aligned Kampuchea as a goal could Beijing make the Khmer cause a worthy one in the eyes of the Southeast Asian countries. And only by expressly disclaiming any role in the communist

---

50. *BR*, March 7, 1983, pp. 15–16.
51. *Ibid.*
52. *Ibid.*, August 1, 1983, p. 18; August 15, 1983, p. 8; September 12, 1983, Supplement, pp. xviii–xxii; October 10, 1983, p. 15. *XHNA*, February 28, April 15, 1984.

activities in Southeast Asia and by actually providing military aid to the non-communist resistance forces could China win the confidence of ASEAN. However, the extent to which Beijing has gone to commit itself to an independent but neutral Kampuchea not allied with China, clearly also reflects China's long-standing image of and policy towards the country. To be sure, the very act of involving ASEAN in China's anti-Vietnamese campaign and of deferring to them the right of initiatives in matters related to Kampuchea also has the effect of committing the ASEAN countries firmly to the cause of the resistance movement and therefore sustaining their united stand on Vietnam. Since the ASEAN countries have been in the fore-front of the international opposition against Vietnam, it is quite clear that if any one of them should decide to give up its hope on the Khmer Rouge or to make concessions to Vietnam, the entire diplomatic pressure on Vietnam would collapse quickly.

Nevertheless, in spite of China's growing sensitivity to the sentiments of the Southeast Asian states in handling the Kampuchean problem and the increasing flexibility of her approach, Beijing has not for a moment changed its basic policy of refusing to accept the status quo in Kampuchea and persisting in an armed struggle against Vietnam. Thus, not only has China consistently defended Democratic Kampuchea's UN seat and rejected any role of the Heng Samrin regime in any international negotiations, but also she has remained adamant on the question of complete Vietnamese withdrawal from Kampuchea as an essential condition of any settlement of the Kampuchean question.[53] Unless and until Hanoi is committed to this and takes concrete action towards its implementation, China has stressed the importance of sustaining a credible armed struggle against Vietnam. Thus, Beijing has objected to all proposals that might weaken either the morale or the strength of the resistance forces. In pushing for a united front, China

---

53. For the most recent reiterations of this position, see *BR*, February 20, 1984, p. 9; *XHNA*, April 15, June 20, 1984.

insisted that the Khmer Rouge must be included if only because
it was the "principal and only effective force resisting Vietnam", and was therefore opposed to the formation of an alternative non-communist movement outside the existing political
framework.[54] At the UN Conference on Kampuchea held in
July 1981, China was even against any resolution or declaration
that would put the Khmer Rouge either in a bad light or on
the same plane as the Heng Samrin regime.[55] Beijing also
declined to accept the proposal made by ASEAN to disarm all
resistance groups and to replace the existing Democratic
Kampuchean Government with an "interim administration"
after the Vietnamese departure, on the grounds that such
measures not only would encroach upon the legitimate rights of
the Kampuchean people but also could only invite the Vietnamese back.[56] While promoting energetically a coalition
government of the three anti-Vietnamese resistance groups,
China in fact repeatedly warned that the distribution of power
among the three groups must not weaken either the fighting
power or the morale of the Khmer Rouge. And in spite of the
initial stalemate in the talks on the coalition government, Beijing
persistently showed both its inability and unwillingness to force
the Khmer Rouge to play second fiddle in the proposed three-
way alliance.[57] After all, China saw the coalition government
of the anti-Vietnamese resistance forces — when it was finally
formed in June 1982 — not as a prelude to a political settlement but rather as the beginning of the development of greater
military pressure on Hanoi which would lead eventually to the
expulsion of the Vietnamese troops from Kampuchea.[58] In

---

54. *ST*, January 6, 1980, p. 3; December 6, 1980, p. 3. *BR*, January
    12, 1981, p. 3; May 4, 1981, p. 3. *FEER*, August 21, 1981, p. 3.
55. *FEER*, July 17, 1981, pp. 13–14.
56. *XHNA*, July 16–17, 1981. See also *FEER*, July 17, 1981, p. 14;
    July 24, 1981, pp. 13–14; August 21, 1981, p. 13.
57. *ST*, January 5, 1982, p. 1; May 15, 1982, p. 2. *FEER*, March
    12, 1982, pp. 12–13; June 4, 1982, p. 10; July 21, 1983, p. 16.
58. Thus, Zhao Ziyang told Sihanouk in July 1982, almost im-

August 1983, Zhao Ziyang told the Australian Foreign Minister, William Hayden: "The unconditional and total withdrawal of Vietnamese troops is the key to a settlement of the Kampuchean issue".[59] But since Vietnam was unlikely to withdraw from Kampuchea voluntarily, Zhao maintained, a compulsory Vietnamese withdrawal "mainly depends on a successful armed struggle against Vietnam inside Kampuchea", and only "substantial support and assistance rendered to...the patriotic Kampuchean forces" could create the condition of an "early, fair and just settlement of the Kampuchean issue".[60] As late as January 1984, Premier Zhao during his visit to the United States said that the conditions for a political solution to the Kampuchean question were not ripe "due to Vietnam's refusal to withdraw from Kampuchea". Therefore, "the surest way to force Vietnam to pull out of Kampuchea is to support the resistance forces in Kampuchea and exert political and moral pressure on Vietnam".[61]

All this suggests that, whatever China's ultimate goals might be with respect to Kampuchea, Beijing expects the international diplomatic pressure only to buttress the political and military position of Kampuchea's anti-Vietnamese movement and eventually to guarantee the separate existence of Kampuchea, not to substitute the fighting in the battlefield. In view of China's legalistic approach towards the entire Kampuchean issue, Beijing apparently believes that any change made to the legal

---

mediately after the establishment of the coalition government, that China expected the anti-Vietnamese forces to "further close their ranks and work in close cooperation" in order to "drive all Vietnamese aggressors out of Kampuchea and win complete victory". *XHNA*, July 17, 1982. See also *XHNA*, July 20, 22, 1982; *BR*, July 5, 1982, p. 10.

59. *BR*, September 12, 1983, Supplement, pp. xxi–xxii. Also, *BR*, August 1, 1983, pp. 9–10; November 16, 1983, p. 44.
60. *BR*, September 12, 1983, Supplement, p. xxiii. Also, *BR*, October 10, 1983, p. 15.
61. *Ibid.*, January 23, 1984, p. 21.

status of Democratic Kampuchea could well weaken its own position, if not also the legitimacy of the resistance movement. Given the inferior military strength of the other two groups combined, any attempt to replace the Khmer Rouge as the focus of rally, or to dictate in advance its ultimate demise before the fighting is over, would certainly have serious demoralizing effects on the entire anti-Vietnamese struggle, if not spell its doom immediately. As long as the Vietnamese troops remain in Kampuchea, any political settlement could indeed only lead to the legitimation of a Vietnam-dominated Indochina. And short of a complete Vietnamese withdrawal, the only option that would leave any hope of resurrecting Kampuchea as an independent nation is armed struggle. In mobilizing international support without at the same time compromising on the necessity of armed struggle, China thus shows clearly her determination to thwart as much as possible Vietnam's aims in Kampuchea and also to meet the Vietnamese challenge in any way Hanoi wants it.

But that is not all. Beijing's determination to keep Kampuchea from Vietnamese domination has been further demonstrated in its Soviet diplomacy launched since 1982. In response to Soviet offers of talks made in early 1982, China identified three major obstacles to the improvement of Sino-Soviet relations, and one of them was precisely Soviet support for Vietnamese occupation of Kampuchea.[62] When the first round of Sino-Soviet talks on the normalization of relations was held in October 1982, Beijing apparently made the removal of these obstacles the precondition of any progress.[63] Since then, China has repeatedly brought up the matter and demanded that Moscow end its policy of support for Vietnam's occupation policy and also use its influence to urge Hanoi to pull out all its troops from Kampuchea. Unless and until this is done, China maintains, Sino-Soviet relations might well deteriorate

62. *Ibid.*, July 19, 1982, p. 3; September 13, 1982, p. 31.
63. *Agence France Presse*, Hong Kong, October 5, 13, 15, 1982.

further.[64] In view of the prolonged nature of the Sino-Vietnamese conflict and the continuing stalemate in the Kampuchean battlefield, this new move made by China is clearly intended to achieve a final breakthrough in her drawn-out diplomatic offensive to isolate Vietnam. Indeed, it is perhaps not too farfetched to argue that China's main purpose of conducting talks with the Soviet Union in 1982 was exactly to remove what Beijing considered to be the mainstay of Hanoi's anti-Kampuchea and anti-China policy.[65] Since the Soviet Union had been the principal ally of Vietnam in the latter's conflict with China, it was quite obvious to Beijing then — and China has actually argued since — that "without Soviet backing, Vietnam could not keep its war machine going. Without Soviet backing, Vietnam could not have the nerve to defy world opinion . . . Without Soviet backing, Vietnam could not stubbornly ignore five UN resolutions".[66] Therefore, if only Moscow could be persuaded to reduce its support for Hanoi, the entire Kampuchea policy of Vietnam would run into serious trouble. This is so particularly because Soviet-Vietnamese relations appear to have experienced some strains during recent years.[67]

However, the persistence with which China has associated Vietnamese activities in Kampuchea with Soviet policy and the importance China has attached to the Soviet involvement in Indochina cannot but continue to betray a genuine and more

---

64. *BR*, March 14, 1983, p. 4; March 21, 1983, p. 12; September 12, 1983, Supplement, p. xviii; October 3, 1983, p. 9; November 14, 1983, p. 9. *XHNA*, April 15, 1984.
65. According to a French Socialist official visiting Beijing in January 1983, China considered the Kampuchean question as "the basic test" of Moscow's good faith in the negotiations. *Agence France Presse*, Beijing, January 4, 1983. Also, *ST*, November 3, 1982, p. 40; December 16, 1982, p. 1; October 15, 1983, p. 44.
66. *BR*, November 14, 1983, p. 9.
67. See Leif Rosenberger, "The Soviet-Vietnamese Alliance and Kampuchea", *Survey*, Autumn-Winter 1983, pp. 213–14, 226–28.

basic anxiety of China about the Soviet threat to her security. Thus, in September 1982, on the eve of the first round of Sino-Soviet talks, the Chinese Party Secretary-General Hu Yaobang told the Twelfth Party Congress that the Soviet support for Hanoi's Kampuchea policy, along with the presence of Soviet troops in Afghanistan and Mongolia, constituted *"grave threats to the peace of Asia and to China's security"*.[68] In late March of 1983, in the midst of the second round of Sino-Soviet talks, China again openly asserted that, as a result of Soviet support for Hanoi's occupation of Kampuchea, "China's security is threatened".[69] In fact, Beijing declared in unprecedentedly unequivocal terms: "The essence" of the three obstacles to improving Sino-Soviet relations "all stem either from the use of military forces by the Soviet Union or by another country with Soviet support, or from the Soviet deployment of armed forces in other countries. They constitute a *grave threat* to the security of China and the peace and stability of Asia".[70] In June, Chinese Premier Zhao Ziyang told the Sixth National People's Congress: "To improve Sino-Soviet relations, the first step to be taken is for the Soviet side to remove the real threat to China's security".[71] In November 1983, just after the third round of talks had been completed, China once again expressed her fears by describing Vietnam as a "pawn" Moscow used to "threaten and attempt to pin down China from the south" and "the knife the Soviet Union has at China's back".[72] As late as July 1984, Beijing declared that the Soviet-Vietnamese alliance formed in 1978 was the "root cause of tension and turbulence in Southeast Asia and gravely threatens the security of Kampuchea, the ASEAN states *and China*".[73]

---

68. *BR*, September 13, 1982, p. 13.
69. *Ibid.*, March 21, 1983, p. 12.
70. *Ibid.* Also, *BR*, September 19, 1983, p. 4.
71. *Ibid.*, June 20, 1983, p. 18. Also, *ST*, October 8, 1983, p. 5.
72. *BR*, November 14, 1983, p. 9.
73. *ST*, July 2, 1984, p. 26.

Indeed, to the extent that the Soviet alliance with Vietnam has been a major contributing factor to the Sino-Vietnamese split and has also accounted for China's uncompromising attitude towards Vietnam, the removal of a hostile power from China's southern flank is essential to rendering a final settlement of Kampuchea acceptable to China. Although Beijing probably does not really expect the Soviet Union to persuade Vietnam to effect a complete withdrawal from Kampuchea, nor is Vietnam likely to change her Kampuchea policy under sheer Soviet pressure, by linking the Kampuchean question closely to the Sino-Soviet détente, China at least attempts to demonstrate to Moscow the unworthiness or unwisdom of supporting Vietnam at the expense of a stable relationship with China.[74] The mere fact that China and the Soviet Union have begun to talk rather than continue to quarrel is certainly expected to create an atmosphere of détente which could well lead to a gradual reduction of Soviet influence in Indochina or a steady erosion of Soviet sympathy for Vietnam.[75]

---

74. The Soviet Union has had to foot a daily bill of US$3 million in keeping the Vietnamese war machine in operation. Rosenberger, *op. cit.*, pp. 213–14.
75. There are signs that in late 1983 Moscow began to encourage Hanoi to improve its relations with Beijing. *ST*, November 2, 1983, p. 44.

7
Hanoi's Diplomacy

Vietnam's strategy has been diametrically opposed to that of China. Realizing the weakness of its legal status in Kampuchea, Hanoi has adopted an essentially moralistic approach towards the whole issue by dwelling painstakingly upon the crimes committed by the ousted Pol Pot regime, and has sought consistently to localize the problem by stressing the stability of the status quo in Kampuchea. In doing so, Hanoi apparently expects to move the Kampuchean question entirely out of the purview of the United Nations or other international organisations and therefore also to keep China at bay. Hanoi declared in early 1979 and many times thereafter that what had happened in Kampuchea was nothing more than a "revolutionary civil war", resulting in the overthrow of a genocidal puppet regime which had long forfeited its moral authority to rule.[1] The new Heng Samrin government, therefore, was not only the "sole legitimate and authentic representative of the Kampuchean people" faithful to their aspirations, but was also in full control of the situation.[2] In fact, throughout 1979, Hanoi even denied the existence of armed conflict in Kampuchea, claiming that there were only operations to mop up "hordes of bandits" infiltrated by foreign countries.[3] Therefore, as Hanoi contended, any

---

1. *RH*, November 10, 1979; *VNA*, September 21, 24; November 6, 24, 1979.
2. *ST*, August 8, 1979, p. 3; *RH*, November 10, 1979; *VNA*, November 24, 1979.
3. *RH*, November 10, 1979; *Sapordamean Kampuchea* (Kampuchean News Agency) (Phnom Penh), November 16, 1979.

attempt to revive the "barbarious Pol Pot regime unprecedented in mankind's history" was "unrealistic", "inhuman", and an "insult" to both the United Nations and the Kampuchean people. Indeed, it could only reflect a sinister scheme engineered by Beijing and other imperialists to subjugate Kampuchea and to oppose Vietnam.[4]

Thus, just as Hanoi had refused to discuss Kampuchea in its bilateral negotiations with China, now it refused to recognize that there was a Kampuchean problem at all.[5] And Hanoi repeatedly proclaimed that any attempt to promote a political solution of the Kampuchean question or to hold international forums on Kampuchea was both unnecessary and unwarranted, and indeed constituted a "gross interference in the internal affairs of Kampuchea".[6] In mid-September of 1979, on the eve of the 34th session of the UN General Assembly, Hanoi declared that the United Nations had no right to include on its agenda issues concerning Kampuchea without the approval of the new Kampuchean government or to discuss these issues without the presence of a representative from the Heng Samrin regime.[7] In fact, to counter the ASEAN-sponsored resolution which called for the Vietnamese withdrawal, Hanoi also put forth a draft resolution calling on all states to "refrain from any action which might infringe upon Kampuchea's right of self-determination, sovereignty, and territorial integrity".[8] Capitalizing on the principle of non-interference in the internal affairs of other states, Hanoi contended that any problem relating to

---

4. *RH*, August 17, November 10, 1979. *VNA*, September 24, 1979.
5. *VNA*, September 13, 1979. Also, *VNA*, September 14, 18, 1979. *RH*, September 12, November 10, 1979.
6. *ST*, August 8, 1979, p. 3. *Agence France Presse*, August 13, 1979. *Voice of the Kampuchean People*, August 21, 1979. *RH*, September 12, 1979. *VNA*, September 13, 21; November 15, 16, 1979.
7. *VNA*, September 13, 21; November 15, 16, 1979.
8. *Ibid.*, September 13, 26, 1979. *The United Nations Chronicle*, January 1980, pp. 39–40.

Kampuchea or other Southeast Asian countries should be settled only by these countries, without foreign intervention.⁹ The adoption of the ASEAN-sponsored resolution in mid-November, as well as of all subsequent resolutions of a similar nature, was therefore flatly rejected by Vietnam as "illegal and invalid".¹⁰

While resisting pressures from international organisations, Vietnam nevertheless did acknowledge the external origin of the Kampuchean situation and continued to assail "Chinese big-nation expansionism and hegemonism" as the real cause of tension and instability in Indochina.¹¹ Throughout 1979, Hanoi's basic argument was that there was no Kampuchean question but only a question of Chinese expansionism in Indochina. It was China which had committed aggression against the Kampuchean people through the Pol Pot regime and therefore threatened the survival of Vietnam.¹² In order to convince the world that China had always had ulterior motives in dealing with Vietnam and had utilized the Pol Pot regime in her southward expansion into Indochina, the Vietnamese Ministry of Foreign Affairs on October 4, 1979, in the midst of the UN debate on Kampuchea, released a White Book entitled *The Truth about Vietnam-China Relations over the Last Thirty Years*, in which Hanoi traced the Chinese ambition to divide the three Indochinese states and to subdue Vietnam back to the 1950s.¹³ In fact, Hanoi claimed that Beijing prevented the Vietnamese first from achieving victory against the French in

---

9. *Vietnam Courier*, December 1979, p. 1. Also, *ST*, August 28, 1979, p. 30; *VNA*, November 15, 1979.
10. *Sapordamean Kampuchea*, November 16, 1979. *VNA*, November 24, 1979; September 24, 1980. *RH*, October 21, 23, 1981.
11. *VNA*, October 5, 1979. Also, *RH*, November 10, 1979; *VNA*, November 16, 24, 1979.
12. *VNA*, October 4, 5, 1979. Also, *RH*, September 12, 1979.
13. *VNA*, October 4, 1979. *The Truth about Vietnam-China Relations over the Last 30 Years* (Hanoi: Ministry of Foreign Affairs, 1979), p. 6ff.

the 1950s, then from "stepping up its armed struggle in south Vietnam" in the early 1960s, and again from "completely liberating south Vietnam" in the 1970s.[14] China's invasion of Vietnam and her continuing support for the Khmer Rouge was therefore merely a "logical development of the expansionist and hegemonist strategy" pursued by China for three decades, with the purpose of "turning Kampuchea into a spring-board for attacking Vietnam" and eventually "conquering Vietnam and the whole of Indochina".[15]

In defending her own position in Kampuchea, Vietnam now openly claimed that the unity of the three Indochinese countries was essential to safeguarding the freedom and independence of each of them.[16] Since, as Hanoi contended, the three Indochinese countries had "continuously been the victims of foreign aggression", and since Vietnam had in the past repeatedly "stood shoulder to shoulder" with her two neighbouring peoples "in their struggle against common enemies", it was only natural and indeed Vietnam's "sacred national duty and international obligation as assigned [her] by history" to come to the help of the Kampuchean people again, this time in order to defeat "Chinese expansionism and hegemonism".[17] The presence of Vietnamese troops in Kampuchea was therefore not only a "legitimate exercise of sovereign rights" which no other nation had a right to interfere with, as it was based on the Vietnam-Kampuchea Treaty, but also "an imperative requirement of the militant solidarity for the defence of the vital interests of the two peoples".[18] Consequently, whereas the

---

14. *The Truth about Vietnam-China Relations over the Last 30 Years*, pp. 11–31.
15. *Ibid.*, pp. 1, 34, 50. See also *RH*, November 10, 1979; *VNA*, November 24, 1979.
16. *RH*, August 17, November 10, 1979.
17. *Ibid.*, August 17, November 10, 1979. *VNA*, November 24, 1979. *Radio Vientiane*, January 7, 1980.
18. *RH*, November 10, 1979; *VNA*, November 24, 1979; *Radio Vientiane*, January 7, 1980.

Vietnamese troops would be withdrawn only upon the request of the new Kampuchean government and following the elimination of the Chinese threat, Hanoi also expressed its determination to remain "closely united" with Kampuchea and Laos in face of any future common enemies.[19] As if to remind the world of the predominant position it had firmly established in Kampuchea and therefore the necessity of accepting the status quo, Hanoi in its official statements made on the issue throughout 1979 and 1980 almost constantly proclaimed: "The situation in Kampuchea is irreversible".[20] Apparently Vietnam calculated that, given the fait accompli in Kampuchea and her own intransigence on the issue of troop withdrawal, it was only a matter of time that the new regime would be accepted by the international community.

In fact, Hanoi was so convinced of its moral duty to salvage Kampuchea from internal degeneration and external threat, and so confident of the prospect of stabilizing the situation in Kampuchea and legitimizing the Heng Samrin government, that it saw no need even to discuss the matter with the Southeast Asian states which were most concerned with the matter, and did not hesitate to adopt a threatening attitude towards them throughout 1979. Thus, as early as July, Vietnam warned the ASEAN countries that criticism of her Kampuchea and refugee policies would "cause difficulties" and increase tension in the region.[21] In mid-September, immediately before the UN General Assembly meeting, Vietnam attacked the ASEAN countries for

---

19. *RH*, August 17, November 10, 1979. *VNA*, November 24, 1979. See also *ST*, August 14, 1979, p. 1; July 19, 1980, p. 34. *RH*, October 3, 4, 1980.

20. For instance, *RH*, November 10, 1979; *Sapordamean Kampuchea*, November 16, 1979. *VNA*, August 10, September 14, 21, November 16, 24, 1979. *Radio Vientiane*, January 7, 1980; *Nation Review* (Bangkok), May 11, 1980. Also, *ST*, July 1, 1980, p. 4.

21. *ST*, July 4, 1979, p. 1.

tabling the Kampuchean issue on the UN agenda and accused them of "following the Chinese expansionists and the U.S. imperialists against the three Indochinese peoples" and "brazenly meddling in the internal affairs of Kampuchea".[22] Hanoi's Deputy Foreign Minister Phan Hien even summoned the ASEAN ambassadors in Hanoi and warned them that if their home governments persisted in their hostile attitude on Kampuchea, there would be "confrontation" between Indochina and ASEAN.[23] After the adoption of the ASEAN-sponsored resolution in the United Nations in mid-November, Hanoi branded the ASEAN countries as "reactionaries" who acted as a "mouthpiece for the Peking expansionists".[24] Singapore, which had been most outspoken against Vietnam, was duped as "the Lee clique" and "a Trojan horse for Peking", not only "voluntarily amplifying all the allegations uttered by the Peking reactionaries" but also "seeking to lure other Southeast Asian nations into selling out their independence and sovereignty".[25] In December, Radio Hanoi, commenting on the ASEAN Foreign Ministers' meeting, warned that it would be "in the interest of the ASEAN states" if they accepted the status quo in Kampuchea as "a practical situation" and a basis for improving their relations with the Indochinese states.[26]

In early 1980, after realizing her growing isolation at both the global and regional levels, as well as confronted with stubborn resistance from the Khmer Rouge on the battlefield, Vietnam in a change of mind decided to seek a dialogue with the ASEAN countries directly. Thus, in a joint communique issued on January 5 by the Indochinese Foreign Ministers' Conference,

---

22. *RH*, September 15, 1979.
23. *Ibid.*
24. *VNA*, October 11, 1979. Also, *RH*, November 11, 15, 1979.
25. *Nhan Dan*, September 16, 1979; *VNA*, November 1, 1979; *RH*, November 11, 1979.
26. *ST*, December 23, 1979, p. 1. *VNA*, December 19, 1979.

Hanoi expressed its desire to establish a "permanent friendly relationship" with other countries in the region and proposed an "exchange of views" between individual Indochinese states and other Southeast Asian countries in order: (1) to conclude "bilateral non-aggression treaties" based on the principles of respecting each country's independence, sovereignty and territorial integrity, non-use of military force in their mutual relations, and non-interference in each other's internal affairs; (2) to discuss and implement the idea of setting up a region of peace, neutrality and stability in Southeast Asia.[27] Confining its attention strictly to Southeast Asia and without mentioning China or the Kampuchean situation at all, the Vietnamese proposal was clearly aimed at blunting the international pressure and undercutting China's diplomatic efforts, and at the same time manoeuvring the ASEAN states into accepting the status quo in Kampuchea. And Hanoi's Foreign Minister Nguyen Co Thach was sent to Malaysia, Thailand, and Indonesia in the spring for the specific purpose of promoting the acceptance of these ideas.[28]

Once set out to woo the ASEAN states, Hanoi also spared no efforts in capitalizing on their long-standing fears of China. Claiming that the Chinese expansionists and hegemonists constituted the "traditional", "long-term" and therefore "permanent" threat to the region,[29] and reminding other Southeast Asian countries of the untrustworthiness of the large ethnic Chinese communities and the activities of communist parties in the region,[30] Hanoi repeatedly told the ASEAN countries that they were also the "targets of Chinese expansionism and hegemony" and therefore should not "allow themselves to be

---

27. *Radio Vientiane*, January 7, 1980.
28. *Nation Review* (Bangkok), May 11, 22, 1980. *Bangkok Post*, May 24, 1980. *Radio Kuala Lumpur*, May 10, 1980.
29. *Radio Vientiane*, January 7, 1980; *Bangkok Post*, May 24, 1980.
30. *Bangkok Post*, May 24, 1980. Also, *RH*, June 27, 1981; *VNA*, July 3, 1981.

exploited by China".[31] In fact, Hanoi argued that since the Kampuchean issue originated from China's ambition to dominate Indochina, it was essentially a problem between China and the Indochinese countries and should not affect Vietnam's relations with other Southeast Asian countries.[32] By involving the ASEAN states in the Sino-Vietnamese conflict, China was therefore promoting confrontation between Vietnam and other Southeast Asian states and "pitting the ASEAN countries against the three Indochinese countries in order to weaken the latter and destabilize the former", thereby paving the way for Beijing's expansion and conquest in the region.[33] Repeatedly proclaiming that Vietnam was in Kampuchea because of the threat from China, Hanoi also maintained that the Chinese threat was the "only factor" leading to Vietnam's intervention and that Vietnamese troops would not "stay there for even one day longer" once this threat was removed.[34] The ASEAN countries should therefore put pressure on China rather than on Vietnam in order to find a solution to the Kampuchean problem.[35]

In a concrete move to dissociate the ASEAN states from China on the issue of Kampuchea, Hanoi in late May of 1980 made a proposal specifically to Thailand to sign a treaty of non-aggression and at the same time urged her to establish contacts with the Heng Samrin regime in order to ensure peace along the Thai-Kampuchean border. Pledging never to invade Thailand, Vietnam's Foreign Minister Nguyen Co Thach in fact said in Bangkok that if Thailand agreed to maintain neutrality and to

31. *Radio Vientiane*, January 7, 1980; *RH*, July 18, 1980. Also, *FEER*, July 25, 1980, p. 8.
32. *Radio Vientiane*, January 7, 1980.
33. *Ibid.*; *Bangkok Post*, May 24, 1980; *RH*, July 18, 1980; *Vietnam Courier*, August 1980, p. 2.
34. *Nation Review* (Bangkok), May 11, 1980; *Agence France Presse*, Jakarta, June 21, 1980.
35. *Agence France Presse*, Jakarta, June 21, 1980; *ST*, June 30, 1980, p. 28.

make peace with Kampuchea, on the basis of respect for each other's "legitimate interests", Hanoi was prepared to "do everything, bilaterally and internationally" to guarantee Thailand's sovereignty, territorial integrity and stability.[36] In mid-July, the Indochinese Foreign Ministers' Conference made a formal proposal which called for: (1) the signing of either a bilateral or a multilateral treaty of non-aggression and non-interference between Thailand on the one hand and the three Indochinese states on the other; (2) the signing of a similar treaty of peaceful coexistence between the ASEAN states and the Indochinese countries, but on a bilateral basis. Vietnam also presented a four-point plan for reducing the growing tension along the Thai-Kampuchean border. The plan called for: (1) the creation of a demilitarized zone along the border; (2) the removal of refugee camps from the border areas; (3) direct consultation between Kampuchea and international relief agencies on aid matters; and (4) direct or indirect talks between Thailand and the Heng Samrin regime.[37]

The immediate objectives of the above offers were clearly to deprive the Khmer Rouge forces of their sanctuaries in Thailand and therefore their vital sources of manpower and material supply, and at the same time to obtain Bangkok's de facto recognition of the Heng Samrin regime. It is quite obvious that if Thailand could be persuaded to compromise, the Kampuchean question would be almost instantly resolved and the resistance movement effectively eliminated. But the general rationale of Hanoi's overall strategy was now also clear. To insist on a dialogue strictly within the Southeast Asian context was to effectively exclude China from any say on the Kampuchean question. Yet to claim that the Kampuchean problem existed only between China and the Indochinese states was also to deny ASEAN the right of intervention. As a matter

---

36. *Bangkok Post*, May 22, 1980.
37. *Vietnam Courier*, August 1980, pp. 2–3, 5; *ST*, July 19, 1980, p. 1.

of fact, in tying Vietnam's occupation of Kampuchea to Beijing's threat, Vietnam sought to deepen ASEAN's suspicions of China and thereby to generate greater regional pressure on China to make concessions. In seeking a pledge of non-aggression and non-interference from the ASEAN states in their relations with the Indochinese states without allowing prior discussion on Kampuchea, Hanoi actually demanded full recognition of the new regime. And in pressing for bilateral contacts between the two groups of states on an equal basis, Hanoi expected not only to elevate the status of the Heng Samrin regime but also to undermine the united front of the ASEAN states by winning them over to its side individually.

Unable to make any progress in its initiatives towards Thailand or break the common stand of ASEAN, the Summit Conference of the Indochinese Foreign Ministers in a further departure from its hard-line stance proposed in late January of 1981 a two-stage plan consisting of a regional conference followed by an international conference. The regional conference would be held between the three Indochinese states and the five ASEAN countries to discuss "questions of mutual concern" which presumably could now include the Kampuchean issue. Then, an international conference involving the United States, China, and other major powers would be held to "recognize and guarantee" the settlement reached during the regional conference.[38] It was even announced that Laos would represent the Indochinese states in conducting preliminary consultation with the ASEAN states. Moreover, the Conference for the first time dropped any reference to the "irreversible" character of the Kampuchean situation.[39] It also declared that Vietnam would withdraw "a number of" her troops immediately if and when Thailand stopped making her territory available to the Khmer Rouge and refrained from supplying

---

38. *VNA*, January 28, 1981; *FEER*, January 30, 1981, pp. 12–13.
39. *VNA*, January 28, 1981. Also, *FEER*, February 6, 1981, p. 8.

them with food and weapons.[40] In May, the Laotian foreign minister was sent to Indonesia, Malaysia, and the Philippines to propagate the proposal.[41]

Hanoi's new proposal was apparently made to accommodate the ASEAN states' insistence on an international framework for a final solution of the Kampuchean problem, as well as their concern for the continuing presence of Vietnamese troops in Kampuchea. Since it was made only after the UN decision to hold a special international conference on Kampuchea, Hanoi's intention to abort the UN conference was also obvious. In fact, the gist of the whole plan clearly lay in the regional conference, the success of which was to precede the holding of the proposed international conference. And in a number of official pronouncements made throughout the first half of 1981, the three Indochinese states repeatedly declared that Southeast Asian affairs must be settled only by Southeast Asian countries, without interference from outside.[42] It was perhaps also no accident that a general election was held in Kampuchea in early May with the apparent aim of buttressing the legitimacy of the Heng Samrin regime.[43]

In a memorandum sent to the UN Secretary-General at about the same time, the three Indochinese states protested that the holding of any international conference on Kampuchea not only constituted an "intolerable interference" in the internal affairs of the Kampuchean people and an "imposition of foreign views on the Indochinese countries", but also could only "pave the way for outside interference in regional affairs" and hinder their own consultation with ASEAN.[44] Vietnam's insistence on a

---

40. *FEER*, February 6, 1981, p. 8; *ST*, January 30, 1981, p. 36; *VNA*, January 28, 1981.
41. *RH*, April 27, 1981. *Radio Vientiane*, May 4, 19, 1981.
42. *VNA*, January 28, 1981. *Radio Phnom Penh*, January 31, 1981. *RH*, April 27, May 9, 1981. *Radio Vientiane*, July 13, 1981.
43. *FEER*, May 8, 1981, pp. 15–16.
44. *ST*, May 23, 1981, p. 38. Also *RH*, May 9, 1981; *Bangkok Post*, June 6, 1981.

regional framework for the solution of the Kampuchean conflict
was presumably aimed not only at keeping China out of any
settlement that might be reached eventually, but also at reducing
the entire issue to manageable proportions. Indeed, in view
of China's adamant stance, the Kampuchean issue could only
be resolved on Hanoi's terms without China's participation.
And apparently if the ASEAN states could be brought to
recognize the reality of the Kampuchean situation, there would
be no need to deal with China at all. Viewed in this light,
Hanoi's indication of its readiness to discuss the issue of troop
withdrawal was clearly aimed at removing the very raison d'être
of holding an international conference on Kampuchea. By
offering Thailand a partial withdrawal of her troops in exchange
for a demonstration of genuine neutrality on Bangkok's part,
Vietnam was in fact putting new pressure on Thailand to make
concessions and also expected the other ASEAN countries to
do the same.

In late August, Hanoi having again failed to break the
stalemate between ASEAN and itself, and being newly condemned by the UN Conference on Kampuchea, the Vietnam-
backed Heng Samrin regime in another gesture to placate
ASEAN proposed to include explicitly in the suggested regional
conference the issue of troop withdrawal, which had been the
stumbling block between Vietnam and her non-communist
neighbours, and the issue of disarming all resistance forces,
which had been a subject of disagreement between ASEAN and
China.[45] In late September of 1981, the Laotian delegate to the
United Nations, on behalf of the three Indochinese states, further expanded the scope of the proposed dialogue with ASEAN
by enunciating seven "principles of peaceful coexistence" which
allowed the two groups of states to discuss virtually all issues
of common concern, including even the delineation of territorial
waters, economic zones and offshore islands in the South China

---

45. *ST*, August 28, 1981, p. 3. For disagreements between China and
    ASEAN, see *FEER*, July 24, 1981, pp. 13–14.

Sea.[46] Apparently to counter the establishment of a standing committee of the UN Conference on Kampuchea, the new proposal also called for the establishment of a permanent body in charge of the "dialogue and consultation" between the two groups of countries, in order to "facilitate contact" before the ASEAN countries were ready for a regional conference.[47]

In the ensuing months, the three Indochinese states repeatedly urged the ASEAN countries to begin the dialogue.[48] The semi-annual conference of the Indochinese Foreign Ministers held in mid-February of 1982 in fact expressed the readiness of the three countries to hold talks with ASEAN "directly or indirectly, bilaterally or multilaterally" in order to settle their differences.[49] In late February, the Laotian ambassador to Thailand further declared that the three Indochinese states were prepared to talk with any ASEAN country about the Kampuchean problem without any preconditions. He also said that the three Indochinese countries were ready to withdraw some Vietnamese troops from Kampuchea, but before doing so, the ASEAN countries must start talking to them or their Laotian representatives.[50] Apart from Hanoi's eagerness to dissipate much of the ill-feelings between itself and ASEAN, presumably any formal dialogue between ASEAN and Indochina as a bloc, or between Kampuchea and any ASEAN member, would still imply a de facto recognition of either the separate and corporate identity of Indochina or the legitimacy of the Heng Samrin regime. And as long as Indochina was placed on the same footing as ASEAN in all the proposed negotiations, the very beginning of such a dialogue would cer-

---

46. *VNA*, September 29, 1981.
47. *Ibid.; VNA*, October 13, 1981.
48. *RH*, October 7, 1981; *VNA*, October 17, 1981; *Sapordamean Kampuchea*, March 20, 21, 1982.
49. *VNA*, February 18, 1982.
50. *Voice of Free Asia* (Bangkok), February 25, 1982. Also, *RH*, February 21, 1982.

tainly signify a softening of ASEAN's position on Kampuchea, thereby leading to the erosion of the international opposition to Vietnam.

These new initiatives, however, did not convince ASEAN of Vietnam's peaceful intentions in the region. Confronted with the emergence on June 22, 1982 of a coalition government of all anti-Vietnamese resistance forces, the three Indochinese foreign ministers, at another conference held in early July, further modified their tough stand by proposing to hold a small-scale international conference on Kampuchea which fell short of the original ASEAN proposal. The conference was to be attended by the three Indochinese states, the five ASEAN states, and the five UN Security Council members, plus India and Burma.[51] The Indochinese foreign ministers also declared that Vietnam would pull out unilaterally and unconditionally some of her troops in Kampuchea as "an act of goodwill" to ASEAN.[52] By attempting to satisfy ASEAN's consistent demand for a truly international conference and for Vietnamese withdrawal from Kampuchea, Hanoi apparently hoped to appear accommodative enough for at least some ASEAN countries to reconsider their support for the Khmer coalition government. Just before Hanoi's Foreign Minister Nguyen Co Thach began his tour of three ASEAN states in mid-July, Hanoi in fact announced that six units of its troops had already been withdrawn from Kampuchea and promised that the withdrawal process would continue if Thailand responded positively to the Vietnamese action and if the "state of security and stability" on the Kampuchean-Thai border permitted.[53]

To demonstrate further that Vietnam had no intention to stay in Kampuchea permanently, in late February of 1983, the Summit Conference of Indochinese Foreign Ministers made a

---

51. *RH*, July 7, 1982.
52. *Ibid*.
53. *Radio Phnom Penh*, July 17, 1982. Also, *ST*, July 19, 1982, p. 1; July 25, 1982, p. 5.

new concession by announcing that Vietnam would effect an unilateral partial withdrawal on an annual basis from 1983 onwards.[54] This was followed in early March by a new proposal made by Hanoi at the Non-Aligned Conference in New Delhi for negotiations between the ASEAN nations and only two Indochinese nations, i.e., Vietnam and Laos, without either the Heng Samrin or the Sihanouk regimes.[55] In early May, Hanoi announced specifically that it would withdraw one division and six brigades of its troops from Kampuchea by the end of the month and even invited Western journalists to Phnom Penh to witness the withdrawal of the first batch of 1,500 Vietnamese troops.[56] This was followed by another Vietnamese proposal made in mid-May to hold talks between representative nations of ASEAN and Indochina, namely Singapore, Malaysia, and Indonesia for ASEAN, and Vietnam and Laos for Indochina.[57] All these novel and impressive diplomatic initiatives, which did strike some responsive chords in certain ASEAN capitals, were apparently designed to break the prolonged deadlock between Vietnam and the ASEAN nations without, however, altering the status quo in Kampuchea. By effecting an unilateral troop withdrawal plan on a periodical basis, Vietnam presumably hoped to placate the ASEAN states and to remove the raison d'être of their continuing opposition to Vietnam. By excluding both the Sihanouk and the Heng Samrin regimes simultaneously from participation in such negotiations, Hanoi intended to save the ASEAN states from the embarrassment of having to deal with an unacceptable regime and therefore finally remove the stumbling block to a dialogue between the two sides.

In early October of 1983, just before the UN General Assembly took a vote on the membership credentials of

---

54. *VNA*, February 23, 1983.
55. *ST*, March 11, 1983, p. 1
56. *Ibid.*, May 3, 1983, p. 3; May 14, 1983, p. 1.
57. *FEER*, May 26, 1983, p. 16.

Kampuchea and the draft resolution proposed jointly by ASEAN and other states condemning Vietnamese occupation of Kampuchea, Hanoi's Foreign Minister Nguyen Co Thach reportedly offered his ASEAN counterparts a trade-off over Kampuchea, according to which Vietnam would drop her efforts to unseat Democratic Kampuchea at the UN if the ASEAN states would refrain from demanding the withdrawal of Vietnamese troops from Kampuchea.[58] Apparently Hanoi sought to obtain at least a de facto acceptance of the status quo in Kampuchea rather than continue to fight a losing diplomatic battle at the United Nations. Indeed, by conceding the UN seat to Sihanouk's government in exchange for cancellation of the ASEAN demand for Vietnamese troop withdrawal, Hanoi could not lose anything that it had not already lost diplomatically but would win at least the valuable, though still tacit, recognition of its right to stay in Kampuchea.

Having failed once again to convince ASEAN of its good intentions, Nguyen Co Thach during his visit to Australia in March 1984 somewhat downplayed the theme of "Chinese threat" by declaring that the elimination of the Khmer Rouge as a military and political force was the top priority in any talks on the Kampuchean problem.[59] By attempting to strike a responsive chord among the ASEAN states and by giving the impression that Vietnam was more accommodative to the other two groups of the Kampuchean coalition government, Hanoi clearly sought to divide the resistance movement and to sow new seeds of discord between China and ASEAN. Presumably, if the Khmer Rouge could be weakened, whether politically or militarily, the single greatest obstacle to Vietnam's complete domination of Kampuchea would be removed.

However, while there has been a steady and significant modification of Vietnam's policy and posture on Kampuchea since 1979, it is also noteworthy that in wooing ASEAN, Hanoi

---

58. *ST*, October 3, 1983, p. 1.
59. *Radio Australia*, March 16, 1984.

has stuck unswervingly to its basic position of considering Kampuchea essentially within its sphere of influence and therefore a closed issue, and has firmly turned down every suggestion made by the ASEAN states to alter the status quo. Thus, in rejecting the Kuantan Principle worked out by Indonesia and Malaysia which called for the neutralization of Kampuchea from all big powers and was therefore close to a de facto acceptance of a Vietnam-dominated Kampuchea, Hanoi's Foreign Minister Nguyen Co Thach in fact declared in May 1980: "The three Indochinese countries must constitute a *single entity* which cannot be distinguished. No one state can be separated from it to become a buffer".[60] While agreeing to effect a partial withdrawal of its troops from Kampuchea, first under specified conditions, then without any condition, and eventually on an annual basis, Hanoi has insisted that complete withdrawal could be made only when the Chinese threat is removed.[61] And since January 1981 Hanoi has repeatedly proclaimed that China's threat can be removed only when Beijing signs bilateral treaties of non-aggression and non-interference with all the three Indochinese states, which is tantamount to China's de jure recognition of the Heng Samrin regime.[62] As a matter of fact, all the diplomatic manoeuvres conducted by Hanoi have been aimed at inducing acceptance, directly or indirectly, of Vietnam's dominant position in Kampuchea, and no solution short of full recognition of the Heng Samrin regime appears acceptable to Hanoi. Thus, in all the proposed talks between the Indochinese states and the

---

60. *Bangkok Post*, May 24, 1980.
61. *Vietnam Courier*, November 1980, p. 29; *FEER*, February 6, 1981, p. 8; February 12, 1982, p. 39; April 23, 1982, p. 44; June 25, 1982, pp. 8–9. *ST*, July 19, 1980, p. 34; January 30, 1981, p. 36; July 29, 1982, p. 38. *VNA*, February 23, 1983; *RH*, April 29, 1983; May 11, 1984. *Radio Jakarta*, March 12, 1984.
62. *VNA*, January 28, February 18, 1981; October 8, 1983. *Agence France Presse*, May 5, 1982; *RH*, July 7, 1982. *ST*, July 21, 1982, p. 40.

ASEAN countries, Vietnam has insisted that either the Heng Samrin regime be fully represented or the three Indochinese nations be treated as a single, integrated bloc, and both Hanoi and Phnom Penh have firmly refused to have any dealings with any of the Khmer resistance groups at all.[63] Even the most recent proposal for negotiations without both Sihanouk's government and the Heng Samrin regime would, if accepted by the ASEAN states, have the effect of grouping the two rival regimes into the same category, thereby either undermining the international standing of the former, or increasing the professed legitimacy of the latter.

Moreover, Hanoi has consistently demanded that the Kampuchean question be discussed and settled only in a regional framework.[64] Even when Vietnam finally agreed to a more broadly based international conference in mid-1982, the conference as Hanoi proposed was to be convened specifically on the principle that "regional problems should be discussed and resolved by the countries in the region without infringing upon the sovereignty or interfering in the internal affairs of each country", which would continue to exclude Chinese participation in any discussion of Kampuchea and to rule out any alteration of the status quo in Kampuchea.[65] In fact, in February 1983, the Summit Conference of Indochinese Foreign Ministers held in Vientiane once again reaffirmed the irreversible nature of the Kampuchean situation by declaring: "The history of the three peoples' struggles...shows that military alliance among them is a *law* of development of the three countries' revolution.... Whenever solidarity is jeopardized, each country's in-

---

63. *ST*, August 28, 1981, p. 3; July 21, 1982, p. 40. *Sapordamean Kampuchea*, October 17, 1981. *Voice of Free Asia* (Bangkok), February 25, 1982. *RH*, July 7, 1982; *FEER*, May 26, 1983, pp. 19–20. *VNA*, January 29, 1984.
64. *ST*, April 17, 1981, p. 36; May 8, 1981, p. 2; July 20, 1981, p. 36.
65. *RH*, July 7, 1982; *Sapordamean Kampuchea*, October 28, 1983. Also, *ST*, July 10, 1982, p. 14.

dependence is in danger''.[66] As late as October 1983, Vietnam's Foreign Minister Nguyen Co Thach proclaimed that Vietnamese troops would stay in Kampuchea "for at least five more years" in order to "prevent the return of the Khmer Rouge''.[67]

While Vietnam's stance and policy on Kampuchea has been in complete accord with her traditional perception of that nation and her security needs, Hanoi's determination to perpetuate its domination in Kampuchea and to eliminate the Khmer resistance was further shown in its continuing escalation of the military operation in Kampuchea and its readiness to use force or threat of force repeatedly against Thailand. While small-scale raids by Vietnamese army units into Thai territory in hot pursuit of the Khmer guerrillas have been a recurrent phenomenon since early 1979, on June 24, 1980, in a move apparently designed to teach Thailand a lesson for pursuing a pro-Khmer and pro-China policy, as well as to halt the mass repatriation of Kampuchean refugees back to Kampuchea, a Vietnamese unit of 2,000 men moved into Thailand and clashed with Thai forces for three straight days in the heaviest fighting ever along the Thai-Kampuchean border, during which tanks and artillery pieces were used and two Thai aircraft were in fact shot down.[68] In January 1981, Hanoi again launched two major armed incursions into Thailand, and fought fierce battles with Thai troops.[69] In early June of the same year, when Thailand intended to repatriate another 90,000 Khmer refugees back to Kampuchea, Hanoi again threatened to take military action against Thailand if the plans were implemented.[70] In February 1982, Kampuchea's Foreign Minister said openly that the Khmer forces "could only be annihilated if Kampuchean

---

66. *VNA*, February 23, 1983.
67. *ST*, October 15, 1983, p. 44. Also, *VNA*, March 27, 1984.
68. *ST*, June 24, 1980, p. 1; June 25, 1980, p. 1. Also, *FEER*, June 27, 1980, p. 10; July 4, 1980, pp. 12–14.
69. *ST*, January 4, 1981, p. 1; January 27, 1981, p. 1. *Radio Bangkok*, January 27, 1981.
70. *FEER*, June 12, 1981, p. 12.

and Vietnamese forces enter Thailand".[71] This was in fact followed by a spate of incidents along the Thai-Kampuchean border, culminating in the intrusion of 300 Vietnamese troops in early March and the killing of a number of Thai patrol police.[72] During his visit to three ASEAN states in mid-July of 1982 following the formation of the coalition government of the anti-Vietnamese forces, Hanoi's Foreign Minister Nguyen Co Thach declared that Vietnam would take appropriate "self-defence measures" if the partial Vietnamese withdrawal led to increased hostility against Vietnam, and warned Thailand specifically that Vietnamese troops had the right to attack Kampuchean resistance forces in Thai territory.[73]

In late March and early April of 1983, Hanoi launched a new round of fierce attacks on the Khmer Rouge forces along the Thai border and did not hesitate to fire artillery shots into Thai territory. As a result, Vietnamese troops clashed with Thai forces for several days and one Thai jet was shot down.[74] In the month of December 1983, Vietnamese troops again clashed with Thai troops repeatedly on land while Vietnamese gunboats opened fire on a fleet of ten Thai fishing trawlers about twenty miles off the southern Vietnamese coast, seizing five trawlers and capturing 130 fishermen.[75] In late March and early April of 1984, Hanoi, in a third major incursion in five years, launched a 12-day cross-border operation into Thailand in pursuit of Khmer forces, using Soviet-made T-54 tanks, 130-mm artillery, and some 400–600 troops. As a result, Thai artillery and air power had to be called into action, resulting in dozens

---

71. *Agence France Presse*, February 3, 1982.
72. *Voice of Free Asia*, February 3, March 3, 1982. Also, *ST*, February 19, 1982, p. 1; March 19, 1982, p. 7.
73. *ST*, July 19, 1982, p. 40; July 21, 1982, pp. 1, 40; July 26, 1982, p. 38.
74. *ST*, April 18, 1983, p. 1; April 20, 1983, p. 1; April 21, 1983, p. 1; April 23, 1983, p. 4.
75. *ST*, December 21, 1983, p. 4. Also, *Bangkok Post*, February 18, 1984.

of casualties on both sides and the downing of another Thai
military airplane.[76] After the incident, Hanoi in fact declared
that, since Thailand had "involved itself militarily with the Pol
Pot clique...to commit crimes against the Kampuchean people", the Kampuchean people "have the right to punish Thai
soldiers in self-defence".[77] The most recent incident occurred in late May and early June, when the Vietnamese navy
repeatedly attacked Thai fishing trawlers off the Vietnamese
coast, resulting in the death of three Thai fishermen.[78] Since
all these attacks or threats of attack were either preceded or
followed immediately by renewals of Hanoi's peace offers, they
were clearly integral to a carrot-and-sick policy designed to induce a policy change on the part of Thailand. And in view of
Bangkok's vital role in the continuing Kampuchean conflict,
presumably if Thailand could be brought to accept the reality
in Kampuchea, whether by persuasion or by force, the entire
united front of ASEAN would collapse and the fate of the
Khmer resistance movement would also be sealed.

Whereas both Vietnam and China were eager and resolved
to outbid each other diplomatically without, however, altering
their basic positions on and goals in Kampuchea, their determination to confront each other militarily was also shown in
the continuing armed clashes along the Sino-Vietnamese border
throughout 1980 and 1981, which apparently no longer had
much to do with either the territorial dispute or the refugee
crisis, but were becoming increasingly a barometer of the
military situation in Kampuchea.[79] It was no accident
indeed that in early July of 1980, following the major Viet-

---

76. *Radio Bangkok*, March 29, April 16, 1984; *FEER*, April 19, 1984,
    pp. 14–15.
77. *RH*, April 5, 1984.
78. *Bangkok Post*, June 5, 1984.
79. China cited 2,000 incidents in the fourteen months after the end
    of the 1979 border war, 114 of which took place in May and June
    of 1980. At least 240 Chinese had been killed, wounded, or kid-
    napped during the same period. *BR*, July 14, 1980, p. 8.

namese thrust into Thailand, a large-scale artillery duel was also fought across the Sino-Vietnamese border.[80] In fact, Beijing on July 5 sent the most severe protest after the 1979 war to Vietnam, threatening to take renewed military action if Hanoi did not stop its "incessant armed provocations".[81] And in the ensuing month or so, Beijing did indeed step up small-scale attacks along the Sino-Vietnamese border.[82] China's promise to come to the help of Thailand was therefore fulfilled. Similarly, in May 1981, when the Kampuchean united front was shaping up, and following the delivery of Chinese arms to the Son Sann forces, a series of large-scale clashes again broke out along the Sino-Vietnamese border, this time apparently at Hanoi's initiative if only to show its displeasure.[83] Since such clashes continued into the months of June, they were also aimed at sabotaging the international conference on Kampuchea scheduled for July.[84] It is also noteworthy that whereas earlier incidences had been skirmishes fought on the company level, the May 1981 clashes involved regiment-sized units numbering as many as 3,000 men on each side and involving the use of heavy artillery and tanks.[85] Since then, violent clashes both along the Sino-Vietnamese land border and in the Gulf of Tonkin have remained a recurrent phenomenon.[86] In mid-April of 1983, China launched a major artillery attack across the land

---

80. *Ibid.* Also, *ST*, July 7, 1980, p. 2.
81. *XHNA*, July 5, 1980.
82. *ST*, August 16, 1980, p. 1.
83. See *XHNA*, May 15, 16, 18–22, 24, 1981. *RH*, May 17, 18, 1981; *VNA*, May 23, 1981.
84. *ST*, June 4, 1981, p. 28; June 9, 1981, p. 3; June 13, 1981, p. 36.
85. *ST*, May 20, 1981, p. 2; May 22, 1981, p. 40; May 23, 1981, p. 1; May 24, 1981, p. 1; May 30, 1981, p. 40.
86. For charges made by the two sides, see for instance, *XHNA*, March 8–10, April 10, June 26–27, July 26, August 28, 1982; *VNA*, April 5, June 3, July 9, August 27, 1982; *BR*, October 24, 1983, p. 8; *RH*, October 22, 1983; *Renmin Ribao*, January 14, 1984, p. 4.

border, apparently in order to curb Vietnam's renewed, massive assaults on the Khmer Rouge forces and Thai border positions.[87] Another sustained spate of border clashes and naval incidents occurred in late August and early September, allegedly at the Vietnamese initiative this time.[88] As recent as April and May of 1984, the two countries again were engaged in a new round of fierce artillery exchanges and ground fighting along their common border almost continuously for two months, as Hanoi increased its military pressure on the Khmer resistance forces and Beijing rushed to their aid.[89] Judging from the nature and frequency of such incidents, the Sino-Vietnamese conflict is bound to continue to assume a strong military character and is also clearly far from over.

87. *ST*, April 19, 1983, pp. 1, 40; April 20, 1983, pp. 1, 4.
88. *BR*, October 24, 1983, p. 8.
89. *XHNA*, April 4, 7, 10, 12, 16, 20, 29; May 1, 10, 16, 20, 23, 1984. *VNA*, April 14, 21, 24, 27; May 12, 14, 19, 23, 1984. *RH*, April 3, 7, 10; May 5, 6, 16, 1984. *FEER*, April 19, 1984, pp. 14-15.

8
Kampuchea and Sino-Vietnamese Relations

Our analysis in the preceding chapters shows that the conflict between China and Vietnam over Kampuchea essentially reflects two divergent patterns of relationship between Kampuchea and her two communist neighbours that have been wrought by geography and history. The resulting differences in perception and policy were reinforced by a profound sense of mistrust between Kampuchea and Vietnam, on the one hand, and between Vietnam and China, on the other, after 1975, as a result of the changing political situation in Indochina. What had been an old problem of security and survival for Kampuchea alone therefore assumed a new magnitude out of proportion to its original significance. The armed conflict in Kampuchea, in fact, soon became an index to, if not also a function of, the Sino-Soviet rivalry. And by virtue of its political and security ramifications, it also quickly came to entangle other countries in Southeast Asia, both diplomatically and militarily. Precisely due to the growing complexity of the Kampuchean issue and its long-term implications, the conflict is no nearer to solution today than five years ago, and the shockwaves it has generated continue to cause vibrations throughout the entire region.

At the centre of the Sino-Vietnamese conflict lies a fundamental clash between two sets of outlooks and goals. Geographically and historically detached from Kampuchea, China has traditionally viewed that country with a degree of apparent indifference and a sense of impotence. With a distinct political and cultural identity of its own, and having evolved as an independent nation after 1954, Kampuchea from the Chinese point of view should at least be entitled to a status equal to the other

157

two Indochinese states. This basic policy of supporting Kampuchea as a separate, independent entity, which has also been the cornerstone of Beijing's Kampuchea policy, was cemented by a relatively long-standing friendship developed over the last thirty years or so between Beijing and Phnom Penh. And throughout the alliance, Beijing, by and large, played the role of a benevolent bigger brother and never assumed an imposing posture in its dealings with Kampuchea. In fact, China was both unable and reluctant to exert a measure of influence on Kampuchea that was greater than Phnom Penh had actually solicited. Clearly aware of the limits of its own power, Beijing from time to time either displayed a conspicuous degree of aloofness from Kampuchea's often openly pro-China leadership and policies, or revealed a measure of powerlessness to render effective assistance to Kampuchea. And all along, Beijing was apparently quite satisfied with a non-communist but neutral regime in Phnom Penh. Indeed, in a region which has been generally hostile to Beijing, a Kampuchea free from foreign domination, though not necessarily subordinate to Beijing, already serves China's interests adequately. Hence China's consistent and in fact enthusiastic vocal support for the independence, neutrality and territorial integrity of Kampuchea, and her unfailing backing for the intractable Prince Sihanouk as its leader even after 1975.

Vietnam's perceptions of and goals in Kampuchea, however, have represented a sharp contrast to China's. If Kampuchea was until recent decades peripheral to China's vital interests, she has always been an immediate and paramount concern of Vietnam, not only because the two countries share common borders, but also because historically Kampuchea was the only potential source of threat to the security of Vietnam other than China. By virtue of her clearly superior power and status among the three Indochinese nations, with a historical relationship of suzerainty over Phnom Penh, and having repeatedly intervened in Kampuchean affairs since the fifteenth century, Vietnam has considered it a matter of course to enjoy a special status in her relationship with Kampuchea and to expect a Khmer regime more or less amenable to her wishes. This basically paternalistic attitude of Vietnam towards her smaller neighbour has been reinforced by Hanoi's undisputed leadership of and almost total domination in the prolonged struggle of the Indochinese communist movement, including the crucial years of 1970–1975. It has also been clearly shown in Hanoi's apparent lack of enthusiasm before 1967 to commit itself to the territorial integrity and political independence of Kampuchea, and in its recurrent and almost constant reference to the "militant solidarity and fraternal friendship" between Vietnam and Kampuchea since then. The demand for a Kampuchea at least closely allied with, if not also subordinate to, Vietnam became all the greater after 1975 precisely because of their far from amicable relationship during the 1950s and 1960s. Indeed, in view of this recent history of enmity between the two nations, a completely independent Kampuchea from Hanoi's perspective is all but synonymous with a hostile neighbour and can only constitute a constant irritant and source of trouble. Therefore, whereas China is willing to tolerate a neutral but not necessarily pro-China Kampuchea, Vietnam cannot be satisfied with anything less than a special relationship with Kampuchea in order to ensure peace of mind.[1]

Vietnam's insistence on a friendly Kampuchea, however, is certainly compatible with China's desire for an independent and neutral Kampuchea, for Beijing, at least prior to 1979, had neither the intention nor the capacity to turn Kampuchea into a forward base against Vietnam. Nor did the Vietnamese quest for a special relationship with Kampuchea necessarily entail an overt Vietnamese occupation before the fall of 1978. Indeed, judging from the disparity in population and power between Vietnam and Kampuchea, and the pervasive influence Vietnam

---

1. As one Vietnamese officials puts it: "We insist on a special relationship, because there is not another example in history of such a relationship where the two peoples shared each grain of rice, every bullet, suffering and victory". *FEER*, April 21, 1978, p. 17.

had developed within Kampuchea during the war years, it would not be difficult for Hanoi to assume a degree of political control over Kampuchea similar to what it had succeeded in Laos in due course. However, Kampuchea's intense distrust of Vietnam and her perennial diplomatic manoeuvring to involve outside powers in her defence strategy clearly upset whatever hopes or plans Hanoi might have had for Kampuchea, and also planted the seeds of discord between China and Vietnam. While Phnom Penh's China policy in the 1950s and 1960s was already based upon a genuine fear of Vietnamese ambitions, the tripartite alliance established in 1970 authorizing a massive Vietnamese presence in Kampuchea made Phnom Penh all the more anxious to secure Chinese assistance in restraining North Vietnamese activities in Kampuchea. Although China's decision to boost the image and status of Kampuchea vis-à-vis Vietnam up to the early 1970s represented a continuation of her well-established policy of supporting an independent Kampuchea, whatever influence she might have exerted on Hanoi for the sake of Kampuchea could not but arouse Vietnamese suspicions of Chinese intentions in Indochina. This is so particularly in view of Vietnam's centuries-old resistance to Chinese influence in Indochina, as well as the diametrically opposed perception Hanoi holds of Kampuchea.

Whether or not Beijing's increasingly close relationship with Phnom Penh actually prompted Vietnam's early reassessment of her ties with China, the relations between the three countries were clearly complicated by developments after 1973, when new but conflicting security concerns were added to old suspicions in a rapidly changing balance of power in Indochina. It so happened that such security considerations were mutually incompatible, as they entailed, from the perspective of the two smaller nations, a greater measure of independence from their respective bigger brothers, but, from the perspective of the two larger nations, a closer relationship with their respective weaker neighbours. It was such non-reciprocal expectations harboured by Vietnam towards Kampuchea and by China towards Vietnam that led the two smaller nations, namely Kampuchea and

Vietnam, to solicit outside support in order to confront their bigger neighbours. But the very act of involving outside powers in turn bred mistrust between Kampuchea and Vietnam and between Vietnam and China. Thus, Hanoi's growing inclination to exert greater influence over the Khmer Rouge quickly collided head-on with the resurgence of Khmer nationalism, as shown in the onset of a series of armed clashes during 1973–1975. Vietnam's new assertive stance on China, and particularly her challenge to China's territorial claims, also alerted Beijing to Hanoi's ambitions in the region. The result was a process of realignment of forces in Indochina, with Vietnam moving closer to the Soviet Union and China leaning more towards Kampuchea.

The end of the Vietnam War and the installation in Phnom Penh of a vehemently nationalistic regime in April 1975 finally destroyed the supporting ground of the precarious triangular alliance. Although Phnom Penh's anti-Vietnamese policy was perhaps essential to reducing the pervasive Vietnamese presence in the country, thereby keeping Hanoi at bay, it was simply unacceptable to Hanoi. Coming immediately after a victory that could not have been won without Vietnamese assistance, it could only be viewed by Hanoi as a clear manifestation of sheer ingratitude that must not be forgiven. To the extent that the new Khmer regime openly aspired to regain control of territories in the Mekong River Delta area which had long been ceded to Vietnam, and was actually responsible for many of the border incidents during 1975–1978, the Kampuchean regime was not merely an irritant to Vietnam, but had actually become a real threat to her territorial integrity and political stability. Moreover, although Phnom Penh's intense hostility towards Vietnam was neither attributable to Chinese instigation nor necessarily supported by Beijing, the longstanding Chinese support for Kampuchea and Phnom Penh's awareness of it must have jacked up the tenor of Kampuchea's anti-Vietnamese rhetoric and the intensity of her anti-Vietnamese activities. Indeed, from the Vietnamese point of view, Phnom Penh could not have dared to turn against Vietnam so suddenly and violently without active Chinese encouragement.

On the other hand, although Hanoi's steady tilt towards Moscow after 1973 was probably still more of a gesture of her determination to pursue an independent foreign policy than specifically directed against China, it was already a bitter pill for China to swallow, particularly in view of the long and intimate relationship between the two countries cemented in blood over thirty years of war in Indochina. Occurring after the tremendous sacrifices China had made in both material and human terms for the sake of Vietnam,[2] and following almost immediately the end of war in the region, it was nothing less than an outright betrayal of an old ally and a blatant display of machiavellism. To the extent that Hanoi did solicit and affirm a special relationship with Laos and at the same time assume an increasingly adamant stance on its worsening territorial dispute with China, and even initiate a long series of discriminatory measures against the one and a half million ethnic Chinese in Vietnam, Hanoi's increasingly intimate ties with Moscow did appear to be deliberately aimed at accomplishing its thinly veiled regional ambitions. As such, Hanoi's anti-China stance and activities also became a real threat to China. Although the Soviets before 1978 probably did not make any firm or concrete commitment to Vietnam vis-à-vis China any more than Vietnam had wanted to join the Soviet bloc, the assurance of Soviet support apparently emboldened Hanoi in dealing with both Kampuchea and China. Indeed, from the Chinese point of view, Hanoi could not have discarded China as its trusted ally so rapidly without Soviet instigation in

---

2. China provided Vietnam with a total of US$10 billion worth of aid during the second Indochina War. *ST*, July 4, 1979, p. 4. Between 1964 and 1971, as many as 300,000 Chinese troops went to Vietnam to man anti-aircraft guns and keep roads and railways open and supply flowing. See *BR*, May 4, 1979, pp. 10–11; July 28, 1979, p. 27; November 30, 1979, p. 14. *XHNA*, July 30, November 27, 1979. *ST*, July 31, 1979, p. 1.

addition to harbouring its own ulterior motives in the entire region.

It was the chain reaction generated by mutual suspicions that steadily escalated the war along the Vietnamese-Kampuchean border and finally pushed China and Vietnam into open conflict in 1978. For Beijing, the Vietnamese expulsion of more than 200,000 ethnic Chinese into China in one single year, and the resulting escalation of tension and violence along the still disputed Sino-Vietnamese land border, clearly pointed to an increasingly unscrupulous neighbour whose unrestrained behaviour must be arrested. If Hanoi's policy towards Kampuchea reflected only its ambitions in Indochina which, though objectionable, were still understandable, its openly anti-China and anti-Chinese activities could not be tolerated because they now directly threatened China's security and stability. To the extent that these acts were committed with open Soviet backing and that Hanoi in the second half of 1978 did somewhat deliberately build up the tension along the Sino-Vietnamese land border, the threat presented by the Soviet-Vietnamese drive against China became an overwhelming one. Hence Beijing's repeated protestations of Soviet-Vietnamese collusion against China and the beginning of Beijing's massive aid and open support for Kampuchea, in order to contain Vietnam. However, the mere fact that China openly sided with Phnom Penh when the Kampuchean-Vietnamese relations were rapidly deteriorating was in turn sufficient to prove to Hanoi the degree of Chinese involvement in the Vietnamese-Kampuchean conflict and the extent to which Beijing wanted to sabotage Hanoi's long-term goals in Indochina. A Kampuchea hostile to Vietnam was already unacceptable enough but still manageable. A Khmer regime openly backed by Beijing in its anti-Vietnamese policies became a serious challenge to Hanoi's security and therefore could only represent a sinister scheme of Beijing to undermine Vietnam's status and strength in Indochina. Hence Vietnam's vehement accusations of China's designs to divide and dominate Indochina. If Hanoi had hitherto attempted only to weaken the Kampuchean regime but not to overthrow it in an outright manner, a decision was apparently made in early 1978 to seize control of Kampuchea by all means, including massive military actions if necessary, in order to put an end to Chinese interference.

Nevertheless, in the steady deterioration of Sino-Vietnamese relations, one continued to detect a clear reluctance on the part of China to exacerbate her conflict with Vietnam or to intervene directly in Kampuchea. This is presumably because both the well-being of the ethnic Chinese in Vietnam and the war in Kampuchea essentially represented situations largely beyond China's control. Thus, in spite of the massive influx of Chinese refugees throughout 1978, China responded only defensively and intermittently to the increasingly tense and violent situation along her land border with Vietnam. There might well have been a persisting hope that Hanoi would therefore be somehow placated. On the other hand, while the escalation of Chinese military aid and the growing Chinese presence in Kampuchea in the course of 1978 clearly would not have been possible without the initiatives of an otherwise fanatically independent-minded regime in Phnom Penh, the increasingly open and firm support China was rendering Kampuchea during the year failed conspicuously to be matched by any concrete commitment to the country's defence. In fact, the repeated hints China gave throughout the second half of 1978 on the limited extent to which she would go to help Kampuchea, as well as the pessimism she openly expressed about the regime's future, should clearly indicate the degree of aloofness or rather powerlessness on the part of China with respect to the Vietnam-Kampuchea conflict. Beijing apparently believed that a combination of open diplomatic commitment and material assistance to Kampuchea should be sufficient to deter Vietnam at least from any overt military action against Kampuchea, thereby preserving the independent status of the latter.

However, the Chinese clearly underestimated Hanoi's determination to regain control over events in Kampuchea and were also too optimistic in their calculations. Precisely because of the apparent Chinese impotence or timidity, Vietnam somehow calculated that the Kampuchean problem could be resolved once and for all at limited risks if Vietnam gave it a final push. With a China tied down by large numbers of refugees in her border areas, and with a massive Soviet presence in Vietnam, Hanoi was also confident that China could not possibly intervene on a large scale even if she wanted to. As Hanoi's repeated attempts at replacing the Khmer regime with one more amenable to its wishes had all failed and there was no prospect for an early victory in the border war, a swift military takeover of the entire country became the most enticing, if not also the only alternative for Hanoi to attain its objectives in Kampuchea. Whether or not the Soviet-Vietnamese Treaty of Alliance, signed in November 1978, had been essentially a product of Vietnamese initiatives, its conclusion following extensive Soviet military assistance throughout the year clearly removed whatever constraints Vietnam might still have in dealing with Kampuchea. In view of the far superior strength she possessed and the short distance between Phnom Penh and the Vietnamese border, Vietnam also believed that the military operation would be a very brief one, with only token resistance from the Kampucheans and entailing minimal cost to herself. And once a fait accompli had been achieved, China would have no choice but to accept the de facto situation in Kampuchea. Hence the high posture which Vietnam assumed when launching the invasion and the haste with which Hanoi formalized its special ties with Kampuchea following the capture of Phnom Penh.

However, on both counts, the Vietnamese had clearly miscalculated. Not only did the Khmer Rouge put up a stubborn resistance by adopting the very guerrilla tactics Vietnam had used successfully against the United States, thereby prolonging the military conflict, but China also intervened on a scale beyond the imagination of the Vietnamese. In fact, Hanoi's invasion of Kampuchea constituted the turning point in Beijing's Vietnam policy which conspicuously hardened after December 1978. Occurring after the drawn-out territorial dispute and the mass exodus of ethnic Chinese from Vietnam, the Vietnamese adventure represented the culmination of a long series of unfriendly acts against China, and also supplied the ultimate rationale for Hanoi's anti-China stance and activities. With 200,000 Chinese refugees already in China, an open aggression against a declared Chinese ally could, in the eyes of Beijing, only reflect Vietnam's insatiable ambitions that had to be arrested at some point and by someone. And the unbridled manner in which Vietnam entered and occupied Kampuchea only made the humiliation to China all the more intolerable. The result of Vietnam's action was also such that any measure less than extraordinary could not have demonstrated effectively China's protest over Hanoi's policy in general and its actions in Kampuchea in particular. Indeed, in launching its own invasion of Vietnam, Beijing did not seek so much to fulfil its pledges to Kampuchea as to penalize Vietnam for her wilfulness and arrogance; and not so much to rescue Kampuchea from Vietnam's conquest, which was after all probably beyond China's means, as to restore China's own face in a hitherto losing conflict with Vietnam. It is only in the context of the above that the bitter and strongly didactic tone of China's accusations makes some sense to lay ears.

However, China's armed intervention was not merely a reaction to an accumulation of her grievances against Vietnam and the situation in Kampuchea. It also served the larger purpose of meeting the more serious Soviet challenge the Vietnamese adventure was believed to have symbolized. And it was this greater menace that actually pushed China over the brink of war. While China saw in Vietnam's increasing hostility towards herself during 1977–1978 an unmistakable Soviet hand, the conclusion of the Soviet-Vietnamese Treaty which formalized the Moscow-Hanoi alliance against Beijing clearly confirmed China's worst fears and further shown her the degree of Soviet penetration in Indochina. From Beijing's point of view, Hanoi certainly would not have committed an open act of aggression against Kampuchea without Soviet sanction. Viewed in this light, the Vietnamese invasion was not merely an aggression against a smaller neighbour, but also a calculated and joint Soviet-Vietnamese undertaking to contain and encircle

China in Southeast Asia. As such, it posed a serious threat to China's southern flank. Precisely because of the extent of Soviet involvement in the Vietnam-Kampuchea conflict and its implications for China, Beijing felt more obligated to support Phnom Penh and also more justified to toughen its stance on Hanoi. And in restraining Vietnamese hegemonism, China believed that she was not only checking the regional ambitions of a smaller state, but also containing the immediate threat of a superpower. Indeed, the degree of preparedness on China's part to cope with the contingency of a full-scale war with the Soviet Union during the 1979 border war could not have been merely for the purpose of resurrecting the Pol Pot regime.

But the Chinese invasion did not render the conflict over Kampuchea more amenable to settlement. Rather, it perpetuated Vietnam's military occupation by providing her with both a pretext and a real need for remaining in Kampuchea. If the high posture China had taken earlier on the territorial dispute and the refugee crisis was at least expected and understandable — as they affected immediately China's sovereignty and territorial integrity, Beijing's military intervention in support of Kampuchea, a country somewhat off the bounds of China's sphere of influence, was from Hanoi's point of view clearly unwarranted and presumptuous. That China should have launched a large-scale war against Vietnam, not as a result of the territorial dispute, nor following the refugee crisis, but only after the Vietnamese invasion of Kampuchea, could not but reflect China's own hegemonistic designs against Vietnam in particular, and her ulterior motives in the region in general. Indeed, had it not been for China's military intervention and material support, the Khmer Rouge probably would not have survived even the initial round of the massive Vietnamese onslaught. By intruding into a region more or less dominated by Vietnam and by obstructing the pursuit of what was viewed as legitimate Vietnamese interests, China in the eyes of Hanoi clearly constituted the most dangerous and immediate enemy of Vietnam and also the major source of instability in the entire Indochina. Precisely because China has intervened on such a large scale, Vietnam has found it all the more necessary and also justified to persist in her policy of occupation. In doing so, Hanoi seeks not only to ensure a Kampuchea subservient to Vietnam but also to put a permanent end to Chinese interference in Indochinese affairs.

The conflict between China and Vietnam over perceptions of and goals in Kampuchea is also reflected in the different strategies and postures they have adopted since the 1979 war. Since Hanoi more or less views Kampuchea as essentially within its sphere of influence and its military intervention as dictated by security considerations, once in there, Vietnam considers the entire issue closed. Hence Hanoi's moralistic approach towards the Kampuchean problem and its adamancy first in insisting that there is no Kampuchean question and then in refusing to participate in any international conference or forum to discuss Kampuchea. By the same token, Hanoi has persistently urged other countries to abide by the principle of non-aggression and non-interference with respect to Kampuchea. Already in control of the country, Hanoi also sees no need to make any concessions to anyone. Hence its repeated and open assertions of the irreversible nature of the Kampuchean situation. Convinced that the Khmer Rouge could not turn the tide militarily even with all the help it could get from outside sources, and that politically time is on the Vietnamese side, Hanoi has in fact unqualifiedly rejected any political settlement that falls short of full recognition of the status quo. Even when Vietnam found it necessary to take the initiative in selling the Heng Samrin regime to the international community after 1980, the approach she adopted was still within a framework that was local in nature, and all the peace offers she has since made have been aimed at undermining the international pressure and keeping the entire issue out of reach to China. While such a strategy is perhaps the only feasible one in order to reduce the Kampuchean question to manageable proportions and to resolve it on Hanoi's terms, it also reveals Vietnam's essentially paternalistic attitude towards her Indochinese neighbours and her determination to keep Kampuchea within her private domain.

China, on the other hand, has always seen Kampuchea as an independent nation and has never recognized Vietnam's inherent right to dominate Kampuchea. Therefore, Beijing has adopted a legalistic approach towards the entire issue and has viewed the Vietnamese intervention in and occupation of Kampuchea as a blatant act of aggression not to be condoned. This explains why she has insisted on treating it as a serious matter of international concern and on seeking an international framework for the solution of the problem. Unable to provide massive military assistance to the Khmer Rouge due to the geographical distance, and aware of the vast disparity in military strength between the Khmer Rouge and the Vietnamese occupation army, China also considers the mobilization and maximization of international political pressure as essential to sustaining the resistance movement and jacking up the cost of Vietnam's occupation. By keeping the entire issue under international spotlight as much and as long as possible, Beijing clearly expects to defeat Hanoi's peace initiatives at bilateral and regional levels, and therefore to prevent Vietnam from legitimizing her conquest. Moreover, in order to ensure continuing support for her Kampuchea policy, China has not only undertaken to promise military assistance to all the ASEAN countries and to promote a united front of all anti-Vietnamese forces, but also has gone out of her way to arm the non-communist resistance groups and to pledge her support for a non-communist regime after Vietnam's withdrawal. These measures have been perhaps necessary in buttressing the diplomatic position and fighting power of the resistance forces and therefore increasing the chances of their eventual victory; they certainly show China's determination to obstruct Vietnam's aim in Kampuchea. But the flexibility they reflect in China's strategy also suggests Beijing's readiness to accept a Kampuchea almost in any colour, as long as it is free of Vietnamese domination.

However, Hanoi's dogged determination since 1979 to maintain its military presence in Kampuchea and to persist in an uncompromising diplomatic stance, despite repeated condemnations by international and regional organizations, is not merely a matter of perception of Kampuchea's relationship with Vietnam, but also reflects a genuine concern about Chinese influence in Indochina. Precisely because Vietnam considers Kampuchea as forming an indispensable part of an indivisible security belt essential to her defence and well-being, China's continuing intervention in the Kampuchean war is nothing less than a direct threat to Vietnam herself. Hence Vietnam's repeated assertions of a Chinese threat through Kampuchea and her insistence upon the removal of such a threat as the precondition for reducing her presence in Kampuchea. Similarly, the firm diplomatic and military backing China has been willing to provide Kampuchea since the 1979 war cannot be adequately explained by her traditional image of Kampuchea, nor is it merely a manifestation of any peculiar Chinese sense of loyalty to a long-time ally. Precisely because China sees in Vietnam's occupation of Kampuchea a more ominous Soviet threat to her own security, unless and until Hanoi withdraws or is expelled from Kampuchea, Beijing's fears of a united Soviet-Vietnamese drive to contain China from the south cannot really be dispelled. Hence the repeated accusations made by Beijing of Soviet hegemonism in Indochina and its insistence on a complete Vietnamese withdrawal from Kampuchea as the prerequisite for an acceptable political settlement of the entire Kampuchean problem.

Since the Sino-Vietnamese conflict over Kampuchea is rooted in conflicting security needs as well as divergent patterns of images and relationships, the prospect for an early solution is virtually nil. On the fundamental strategical level, China simply cannot tolerate the presence of a hostile power in Indochina, much less so when it represents an act of betrayal by a former protégé. In order to ensure a friendly Indochina and a secure southern border, China has in the past lent all-out and unswerving support to the Indochinese peoples during two protracted wars in the region and under much more arduous conditions. There is therefore every reason to believe that she will continue to pursue the same objective today whether the new threat is posed by the Vietnamese or the Soviets. On the other hand,

Vietnam also cannot accept the continuing interference in Indochinese affairs by outside powers, much less by a country which has geographically and historically posed a threat to Vietnam. Nor can she allow a hostile regime in either of her two weaker western neighbours. Indeed, from Hanoi's perspective, the war in Kampuchea represents the final round of a century-old anti-colonial and anti-imperialist struggle which Vietnam has to win in order to bring lasting peace and security to herself. And if Vietnam has fought successfully against the more powerful French and Americans, she is certainly not likely to submit to the pressure of a militarily weaker China.

The incompatibility between these two sets of strategical calculations are well illustrated by the very circularity of arguments and demands made by the two countries: for Vietnam, the removal of Chinese threat must precede any reduction of Vietnamese presence in Kampuchea, but for China, there can be relaxation of pressure on Vietnam only after the withdrawal of the Vietnamese from Kampuchea. Unless and until one party retreats from its position first, there is clearly no way of breaking the circle. Yet neither side can afford or is prepared to make the first move as long as the war in Kampuchea continues, since to do so is not only to concede defeat but also to actually run the risk of allowing its fears to be translated into reality. For China to agree now to stop pressurizing Vietnam is tantamount to accepting the legitimacy of a Vietnam-dominated Kampuchea and acquiescing in Soviet advances in mainland Southeast Asia, whereas for Vietnam to withdraw her troops completely from Kampuchea now is to allow the resurgence of a hostile Kampuchea and to accept China's pre-eminence in Indochina.

As a matter of fact, quite ironically, the militant strategies and defiant postures adopted by Beijing and Hanoi on the issue of Kampuchea have not only reconfirmed but also reinforced their mutual perceptions of threat from each other, which in turn have compelled both countries to persist in a hard-line policy. For Vietnam, China's intransigence has clearly underscored the need to consolidate the interdependence and indivisibility of the three Indochinese nations in defence and other matters. For China, Vietnam's obstinacy has also exposed the glaring vulnerability of her southern borders and therefore the need to minimize it. Thus, if Vietnam before 1978 had desired only a special relationship with Kampuchea and never envisaged a complete absorption of Kampuchea into Vietnam, she is now clearly determined to proceed to complete the conquest of her weaker neighbour. Yet having exhibited her aggressiveness in the eyes of China by this policy, Vietnam is bound to invite continuing pressure from the north, thereby generating a real threat from China. On the other hand, if China before 1979 had only wanted to keep Kampuchea independent from Vietnam, she has no alternative now but to promote an anti-Vietnamese regime in Phnom Penh. In doing so, China also inevitably turns what has previously been merely an ungrateful neighbour displaying pro-Soviet tendencies into a real enemy across her southern border. And as long as China is involved in the Kampuchean war, the Soviet shadow is likely loom large in the region, thereby actually complicating China's security problems in the south.

At the more pragmatic — i.e., diplomatic and military — level, the two sides are also unable to extricate themselves easily from the continuing conflict. Having been on the defensive in its territorial and ethnic disputes with Hanoi, Beijing could not retreat on the Kampuchean question without conceding total defeat in its drawn-out conflict with Vietnam. Already committed to the cause of the resistance movement with extensive investment, China also could not afford to abandon the Khmer Rouge without seriously damaging her own image. This is so particularly at a juncture of delicate balance of forces on the battlefield which could well be upset in Hanoi's favour by any sign of vacillation on the part of Beijing. Therefore, in spite of the little progress made in reversing the military trends in Kampuchea, China's position on the entire issue has remained adamant and consistent since 1979, and she has repeatedly assured Khmer leaders of her unswerving commitment to the cause of resistance. Thus, on November 5, 1982, Chinese

Premier Zhao Ziyang told Sihanouk in Beijing: "China will as always support the Kampuchean people in their struggle against Vietnamese aggression *until they win final victory*".[3] As late as September 1983, Beijing declared: "As long as Vietnamese aggression continues in Kampuchea and the Kampuchean people have not regained their national rights, the Chinese people will not cease supporting their just struggle against aggression *until final victory*".[4] In fact, since the formation of the coalition government in June 1982, Beijing has stepped up its financial and military aids to the resistance forces.[5] As long as the Kampucheans are willing to fight the Vietnamese, China is determined to stay in the war.

Although China does not expect to achieve a miracle by turning the tide of the war in Kampuchea soon, she is at least prepared to wear down Vietnam through a protracted guerrilla war. By continuing to bleed the Vietnamese for as long as possible, presumably China hopes to make the Vietnamese occupation militarily so costly as to render it politically untenable, thereby ushering in a change either in Hanoi's basic policy towards Kampuchea or in its leadership structure which would eventually also bring about a policy reorientation. At the same time, by keeping the anti-Vietnamese resistance movement credible and by expanding its political and operational bases as much as possible, China also seeks as an immediate goal to ensure that the military situation in Kampuchea will not become so unfavourable as to lend any credence to the legitimacy of the Heng Samrin regime. This is also why China has

---

3. *BR*, November 29, 1982, p. 7. See also, *XHNA*, July 20, 1982. According to Prince Sihanouk, Hu Yaobang, the Secretary-General of the Chinese Communist Party, told him in January 1983 that "in four years the coalition government would be triumphantly installed in Phnom Penh". *FEER*, June 16, 1983, pp. 12–13.

4. *BR*, September 10, 1983, Supplement, p. xvii.

5. *ST*, June 24, 1982, p. 1; October 29, 1982, p. 9; November 22, 1982, p. 38; December 14, 1982, p. 1; December 29, 1983, p. 3.

shown such enthusiasm about a coalition government and such generosity in giving military aid to all anti-Vietnamese forces as long as they pledge not to sabotage the entire resistance effort. In fact, as a result of such a strategy, Vietnam has had to increase steadily her troop strength in Kampuchea, from 100,000 in January 1979 to 200,000 in 1981, in addition to the massive build-up along the Sino-Vietnamese land border. Indeed, from the Chinese point of view, as long as fighting in Kampuchea is not over and Vietnam's control over all Kampuchea remains a goal, not a reality, China is still in the process of administering lessons to Vietnam.

If China could not afford to retreat from Kampuchea without serious repercussions on both the fate of the Khmer Rouge and her own international standing, Vietnam certainly sees no reason why she should surrender her gains which are all but firmly secured. Having been in Kampuchea for more than five years, Vietnam cannot withdraw now without admitting the illegality of her occupation all along or allowing the entire edifice of the Heng Samrin regime to go bankrupt. Commanding a clear military advantage in Kampuchea and fearing no direct Chinese military involvement, Hanoi is also in no danger of being forced out of Kampuchea in the near future. Indeed, without a clear victory in Kampuchea or an all-out war against Vietnam, and short of a military conquest, China cannot expect to bring Vietnam to her knees. Thus, in spite of the continuing stalemate in the battlefield, Vietnam's basic position on the Kampuchean issue has also not changed since her occupation began in January 1979. In fact, Le Duan in his political report to the Fifth Congress of Vietnam's Communist Party in late March of 1982 proclaimed: "The special Vietnam-Laos-Kampuchea relationship is a *law* of development of the revolution in the three countries . . . and a firm guarantee for the cause of defending the independence and freedom and successfully building socialism in each country on the Indochinese peninsula".[6] In

---

6. *VNA*, March 29, 1982.

late July, Vietnam's Foreign Minister, Nguyen Co Thach, said in Bangkok: "The realities of the past thirty-five years when Vietnam won wars against the French and the Americans proved that the Indochinese people could not be subjugated".[7] In November 1983, in response to the UN vote condemning Vietnamese occupation of Kampuchea for the fifth time, Nguyen Co Thach said: "Whether there is a voting or not, the stand of the three Indochinese countries and their friends remain unchanged". And he added: "Just as twenty years of voting in favour of Chiang Kai-shek failed to change the situation in China . . . the erroneous UN resolution in the past five years have failed either to reverse the situation in Kampuchea or to prevent Kampuchea's rebirth".[8] As recently as March 1984, Nguyen Co Thach declared in a television interview: "Experiences from the past five years have indicated that...within the next five to ten years...the so-called Kampuchean question will no longer exist".[9] Vietnam apparently believes that by staying as long as possible in Kampuchea, she is sure to emerge victorious in her contest of will and power with China and to turn eventually a fait accompli into a legitimate piece of territory.

Hanoi's determination to wipe out the resistance forces by all means is clearly shown in its increasingly indiscriminate use of chemical weapons during 1981–82 against both the civilians under the influence of the Khmer Rouge and the guerrillas themselves. And this was done in spite of the growing international concern over the matter.[10] Since January 1982, Hanoi has also thrown additional troops into the fighting in western Kampuchea and has launched sustained attacks on all the guerrilla strongholds, including those of the non-communist

---

7. *ST*, July 24, 1982, p. 36.
8. *VNA*, November 9, 1983. See also *ST*, October 28, 1982, p. 40.
9. *VNA*, March 27, 1984.
10. *FEER*, January 15, 1982, pp. 22–23; *ST*, November 7, 1981, p. 40; January 31, 1982, p. 2; March 15, 1982, p. 3.

Son Sann forces.[11] And in spite of the much publicized partial withdrawal of Vietnamese troops in 1983 and 1984, the large-scale dry-season offensives that invariably preceded such withdrawals have given every impression that Hanoi is determined to achieve a breakthrough in the protracted war[12] But that is not all. In order to expand and consolidate its grip on both Kampuchea and Laos, Hanoi has since late 1981 somewhat stepped up its colonization campaign launched in the spring of 1979.[13] Although the precise scale of Vietnamese settlement since the initial influx of 250,000 people in late 1979 cannot be ascertained yet, the nature and momentum of such population migration is revealed at least in part by the removal of the Heng Samrin regime's number two man, Pen Soven, from power in December 1981, allegedly due to his opposition to Vietnam's colonization policy.[14] Meanwhile, to speed up the integration of the three parts of Indochina, Hanoi has steadily improved the communication and road systems linking Kampuchea and Laos with Vietnam, provided considerable

---

11. *FEER*, January 8, 1982, pp. 14–15; February 26, 1982, pp. 14–15; March 5, 1982, pp. 12–13.
12. *ST*, January 19, 1983, p. 4; February 5, 1983, p. 1. *FEER*, February 17, 1983, p. 14; April 14, 1983, pp. 14–15; March 8, 1984, pp. 36–37; April 19, 1984, p. 14; May 3, 1984, p. 20; May 10, 1984, p. 20.
13. *Voice of Free Asia* (Bangkok), November 20, 1981; *FEER*, January 8, 1982, p. 13; May 26, 1983, pp. 18–19. *ST*, August 13, 1982, p. 40; September 24, 1982, p. 40.
14. *FEER*, January 8, 1982, p. 13. See also *ST*, November 5, 1979, p. 32; December 8, 1981, p. 18. According to sources in Bangkok, Hanoi in late 1983 again moved large numbers of Kampucheans to the western border provinces in order to facilitate Vietnamese settlement. The Khmer Rouge claim that since 1979, at least 600,000 Vietnamese civilians have settled in Kampuchea, but Hanoi and Phnom Penh put the figure at around 70,000. *Reuter Dispatch*, Bangkok, October 27, 1983. See also *ST*, October 22, 1983, p. 3; *Bangkok Post*, September 30, 1983, pp. 1, 3.

amounts of economic aid to both Kampuchea and Laos, dispatched hundreds of specialists each year to work in the two countries, and recruited thousands of students to study in Vietnam.[15] In the light of all the above, the original French concept of an Indochina Federation has indeed already "passed into the history" and lost its appeal to Hanoi as Vietnam has claimed, for after the drawn-out military conflict, Hanoi is apparently no longer satisfied nor feels secure with anything less than a thoroughly united entity in the form of a greater Vietnam.[16]

As neither China nor Vietnam is prepared to make any concessions, the outcome of the Sino-Vietnamese conflict over Kampuchea depends to a large extent upon the ability of the Kampuchean resistance forces to withstand Vietnam's growing military pressure and to continue to expand their base of popular support. It also depends upon the successful co-operation of all anti-Vietnamese forces, which is crucial to retaining at least the international diplomatic support the resistance movement has been enjoying. So far the Khmer Rouge has repeatedly thwarted Vietnam's dry-season offensives, including the most recent and hitherto most intensive onslaught by the Vietnamese forces, thereby demonstrating its political resilience and military credibility. It is also remarkable that the otherwise intense mistrust between Sihanouk, Son Sann, and the Khmer Rouge has proven to be much less than their common hatred of the Vietnamese, in spite of the recurrent signs of strains between the three strange bedfellows.[17] If the

---

15. *FEER*, October 6, 1983, p. 50.
16. The original French concept of an Indochina Federation was in fact a loosely associated union of three to five nations led by France, each enjoying substantial autonomy. The current state of affairs in Indochina has clearly already passed that stage. See Ellen J. Hammer, *The Struggle for Indochina: 1940–1955* (Stanford: Stanford University Press, 1954), p. 112ff.
17. *FEER*, June 16, 1983, pp. 12–14; June 30, 1983, p. 15; January

Khmer Rouge can keep up its military performance for another few years, and if the united front between the Khmer Rouge and other anti-Vietnamese forces can be sustained, the political fortune of the Kampuchean resistance movement could well witness a dramatic turn for the better. Conversely, it is also quite clear that failure to attain both of the above two goals can seriously erode the legitimacy and international support of the Khmer Rouge, if not also jeopardize the very survival of the entire resistance movement. Whatever the eventual outcome might be, the cost for Kampuchea as a nation and a people will certainly be tremendous. Indeed, it is both ironical and tragic that a nation which has been so eager to involve outside powers to ensure its security could well be, in the very process of so doing, inviting its own ultimate demise.[18] However, whether or not Kampuchea could in the end regain her independence and vitality, the relations between China and Vietnam will remain strained for a long time, since a final Vietnamese victory over the Khmer Rouge would be a humiliating defeat for China after so many years of commitment and investment, whereas an ultimate victory of the Khmer Rouge would deny Vietnam a valuable piece of territory essential to the formation of a Vietnam-dominated Indochina.

5, 1984, pp. 14–15; January 19, 1984, pp. 32–34; February 9, 1984, pp. 18–19. *ST*, November 18, 1983, p. 3.

18. Prince Sihanouk in fact predicted the eventual demise of the Khmer resistance. *FEER*, June 16, 1983, p. 13.

APPENDICES

1
Treaty of Friendship and Mutual Non-Aggression between the People's Republic of China and the Kingdom of Cambodia

Liu Shao-chi, Chairman of the People's Republic of China, and His Royal Highness Prince Norodom Sihanouk, Head of State of Cambodia,

desiring to maintain a lasting peace and a cordial friendship between the People's Republic of China and the Kingdom of Cambodia,

convinced that the strengthening of good neighbourly relations and friendly co-operation between the People's Republic of China and the Kingdom of Cambodia conforms to the vital interests of the two countries,

have decided to conclude the present treaty in accordance with the Five Principles of Peaceful Co-existence, the spirit of the Asian-African Conference held in Bandung in 1955 and the principles adopted at it, and

have for this purpose, appointed as their respective plenipotentiaries:

for the People's Republic of China: Chou En-lai, Premier of the State Council of the People's Republic of China; for the Kingdom of Cambodia: His Excellency Pho Proeung, Prime Minister of the Government of the Kingdom of Cambodia,

who, having exchanged and examined each other's full powers, found in good and due form, have agreed upon the following:

Article One

The People's Republic of China and the Kingdom of Cambodia will maintain a lasting peace between them and develop and consolidate their friendly relations.

Article Two

Each contracting party undertakes to respect the sovereignty, independence and territorial integrity of the other.

Article Three

The contracting parties undertake to settle any disputes that may arise between them by peaceful means.

Article Four

Each contracting party undertakes not to commit aggression against the other and not to take part in any military alliance directed against the other.

Article Five

The contracting parties will develop and strengthen the economic and cultural ties between the two countries in accordance with the principles of equality and mutual benefit and of non-interference in each other's internal affairs.

Article Six

Any difference or dispute that may arise out of the interpretation or application of the present treaty or one or several articles of the present treaty shall be settled by negotiation through normal diplomatic channels.

Article Seven

The present treaty is subject to ratification in accordance with the constitutional procedures of each of the contracting parties. It will come into force on the date of exchange of the instruments of ratification which will take place in Phnom Penh as soon as possible.

It will remain in force so long as neither of the contracting parties denounces it by notice one year before the expiration of this period.

In faith thereof, the plenipotentiaries of both sides have signed the present treaty.

Done in duplicate in Peking on the Nineteenth day of December, 1960, in the Chinese, Cambodian and French languages, all three texts being equally authentic.

(Signed) Chou En-lai   (Signed) Pho Proeung
Plenipotentiary of the   Plenipotentiary of the
People's Republic of China   Kingdom of Cambodia

2
Treaty of Friendship and Cooperation between the Socialist Republic of Vietnam and the Lao People's Democratic Republic

The Socialist Republic of Vietnam and the Lao People's Democratic Republic,

deeply aware that the special Vietnam-Laos relationship, the unshakable militant solidarity and friendship between the peoples of Vietnam and Laos, the great comradeship between the Communist Party of Vietnam and the Lao People's Revolutionary Party, tempered in several decades of sharing the sweet and the bitter, fighting together and defeating the same aggressor enemy and cooperating and assisting each other in building the country, are a valuable tradition and an invincible strength of the two nations and Parties, a vivid reality and a law of development of the Vietnamese and Lao revolutions;

holding that the strengthening of the ironclad solidarity and lasting relations of cooperation in all spheres between Vietnam and Laos responds to the earnest desire and interests and survival of the peoples of all countries in the task of protecting national independence and building socialism, and is consistent with the interests and genuine national independence, democracy, peace and neutrality of the peoples of Southeast Asian countries and with the interests of the world's peoples struggling against imperialism, colonialism, and neo-colonialism and for peace, national independence, democracy and social progress;

remaining loyal to Marxism-Leninism, continuing to hold high the banner of national independence and socialism, skilfully combining genuine patriotism with proletarian internationalism, endeavouring to protect and develop the special Vietnam-Laos relationship to make the two countries, inherently united in the national liberation cause, remain united forever in national construction and defence;

agreeing on the fact that the independent and sovereign line and correct leadership of the Communist Party of Vietnam and the Lao People's Revolutionary Party, the tradition of cordial solidarity between the two nations, the complete victory of both countries in the struggle against aggressive imperialism, and the objectives of the peoples of both countries struggling for socialism, constitute the fundamentals for the development of the special Vietnam-Laos relationship;

on the basis of the spirit of the Vietnam-Laos joint statement of the Eleventh of February, 1976;

seeking to enhance the solidarity, lasting co-operation and mutual assistance in building and protecting the countries for the sake of each country's independence and prosperity, and to contribute to safeguarding and consolidating peace in Southeast Asia and in the world;

have decided to sign this treaty and have agreed on the following articles:

Article One

Both sides pledge to endeavour to protect and develop the special Vietnam-Laos relationship; unceasingly to strengthen the solidarity, reciprocal confidence, and the lasting cooperation and mutual assistance in all spheres in the spirit of proletarian internationalism and in accordance with the principle of total equality, respect for each other's independence, sovereignty and territorial integrity, respect for each other's legitimate interests and non-interference in each other's internal affairs. Each side will endeavour to educate its entire Party and its entire people constantly to value, protect and foster the special Vietnam-Laos relationship so that it will remain pure and steady forever.

Article Two

On the basis of the principle of safeguarding national independence and maintaining national security, which is the undertaking of the people of each country, both sides pledge to support and assist each other whole-heartedly and to cooperate closely in increasing the capability of defending and protecting the independence, sovereignty and territorial integrity, maintaining the people's peaceful labour, and opposing all schemes and acts of sabotage by the imperialists and foreign reactionary forces.

Article Three

To create advantages for each other and to help each other overcome difficulties and effectively develop each country's material potentialities so as to build a prosperous and powerful country and a happy and decent life, both sides will strengthen the relations of socialist cooperation and mutual interests in agriculture, forestry, industry, communications and transport, the exploitation of natural resources and other economic spheres; will whole-heartedly assist each other in the economic and technical fields and in training cadres; will exchange experts in the economic, cultural, scientific and technical branches and will expand trade relations according to the system of special preferential treatment. Both sides will expand scientific and technical exchanges and cooperation in the cultural, artistic, educational, health, information, press, broadcasting, cinematographic, physical training and sports aspects and in other cultural spheres. Both sides will increase the contacts between the concerned branches of both countries to discuss the implementation of cooperative plans and exchange views on economic building and cultural development.

Article Four

Both sides assert their determination to build the Vietnam-Laos border into a border of fraternal friendship between the two countries on the basis of the treaty on the delimitation of the national frontier between the Socialist Republic of Vietnam and the Lao People's Democratic Republic signed on the Eighteenth of July, 1977.

Article Five

Both sides fully respect and support each other's international line of independence and sovereignty. Both sides will strive to strengthen the militant solidarity and cooperative relations with other fraternal socialist countries; positively contribute together with the other socialist countries and the international communist movement to intensifying their solidarity and mutual support and assistance on the basis of Marxism-Leninism and proletarian internationalism; unceasingly strengthen the militant solidarity, lasting cooperation with, and mutual assistance to, fraternal Cambodia in accordance with the principle of total equality, respect for each other's independence, sovereignty and territorial integrity, respect for each other's internal affairs; support the Southeast Asian people's struggle for national independence and genuine democracy, peace and neutrality; establish and develop the relations of friendship and cooperation with the countries in this area on the basis of respect for each other's independence, sovereignty and territorial integrity, non-aggression against each other, non-interference in each other's internal affairs, equality and mutual interests and peaceful co-existence; support the struggles of the peoples of Asia, Africa and Latin America against imperialism, colonialism, neo-colonialism and racism and for national independence, democracy and social progress; support the struggle of the working class and labouring people in capitalist countries for their welfare, democracy and social progress; and pledge to do their best to contribute to the common struggle of the world's peoples for peace, national independence, democracy and socialism.

Article Six

Both sides will hold regular exchanges of views on the problems related to both countries' relations and on international issues of mutual concern through meetings between the Party and State leaders of both countries, through visits by various official delegations and special representatives, or through diplomatic channels. Both sides will encourage the expansion of relations between the mass organizations of both countries. All problems concerning the relations between the two countries will be solved through negotiations in the spirit of mutual understanding and respect and in a rational and sensible manner.

Article Seven

This treaty will be ratified and will take effect from the day of the exchange of ratification letters. The exchange of ratification letters will be achieved in Hanoi, capital of the Socialist Republic of Vietnam, as soon as possible.

This treaty is valid for twenty-five years and will be tacitly renewed for ten years on each occasion if one of the signatories does not notify the other side through a document of his intention to cancel the treaty at least one year prior to its expiration.

This Treaty was made in Vientiane, capital of the Lao People's Democratic Republic, on the Eighteenth of July, 1977, in duplicate in the Vietnamese and Lao languages, both copies being equally authentic.

On behalf of the Socialist   On behalf of the Lao People's
Republic of Vietnam: Democratic Republic:
(Signed) Pham Van Dong   (Signed) Kaysone Phomvihan

Done in duplicate in the Vietnamese and Russian languages, both texts being equally authentic, in Moscow this Third day of November, 1978.

For the Socialist Republic
of Vietnam:
(Signed) Le Duan
Pham Van Dong

For the Union of Soviet
Socialist Republics:
(Signed) L.I. Brezhnev
A.N. Kosygin

4

Treaty of Peace, Friendship and Cooperation between the Socialist Republic of Vietnam and the People's Republic of Kampuchea

The Socialist Republic of Vietnam and the People's Republic of Kampuchea,

proceeding from the traditions of militant solidarity and fraternal friendship between Vietnam and Kampuchea, which have overcome many trials and become an unbreakable force ensuring the success of each country's national defence and construction,

deeply conscious that the independence, freedom, peace and security of the two countries are closely inter-related and that the two Parties are duty-bound to help each other whole-heartedly and with all their might to defend and consolidate the great revolutionary gains they have recorded through nearly thirty years of struggle full of hardship and sacrifice,

affirming that the militant solidarity and the long-term and all-round cooperation and friendship between Vietnam and Kampuchea meet the vital interests of the two peoples and, at the same time, are a factor ensuring a durable peace and stability in Southeast Asia, and are in keeping with the basic interests of the peoples in this region and contribute to the maintenance of peace,

confident that the Kampuchean people's complete victory under the glorious banner of the National United Front for the Salvation of Kampuchea, the correct line of independence, sovereignty and international solidarity of each country, and respect for each other's legitimate interests constitute a

194

firm basis for the constant development of friendship and cooperation between the two countries,

desirous to strengthen the militant solidarity, the long-term cooperation and friendship and mutual assistance in all fields to consolidate independence, build a prosperous country and a happy life for each people, thus constributing to the maintenance of peace and stability in Southeast Asia and the world, in keeping with the objectives of the non-aligned movement and the United Nations Charter,

have decided to sign this Treaty and have agreed as follows:

Article One

The two Parties signatory to the present Treaty undertake to do all they can to preserve and constantly develop the traditional militant solidarity, friendship and fraternal co-operation between Vietnam and Kampuchea, and mutual trust and assistance in all fields on the basis of respect for each other's independence, sovereignty and legitimate interests, non-interference in each other's internal affairs, equality and mutual benefit.

The two Parties shall do all they can to educate the cadres, fighters and people of their respective countries to preserve forever the purity of the traditional militant solidarity and loyal friendship between Vietnam and Kampuchea.

Article Two

On the principle that national defence and construction are the cause of each people, the two Parties undertake to whole-heartedly support and assist each other in all domains and in all necessary forms in order to strengthen the capacity to defend the independence, sovereignty, unity, territorial integrity and peaceful labour of the people in each country against all schemes and acts of sabotage by the imperialist and international reactionary forces. The two Parties shall take effective measures to implement this commitment whenever one of them requires.

Article Three

In order to help each other build a prosperous and powerful country and happy and plentiful lives for their peoples, the two Parties shall promote mutually beneficial fraternal exchanges and cooperation and assist each other in the fields of the economy, culture, education, public health, science and technology, and in training cadres and exchanging specialists and experience in all fields of national construction.

To attain this objective, the two Parties shall sign necessary agreements and, at the same time, increase contacts and cooperation between the State bodies concerned and between mass organizations of both countries.

Article Four

The two Parties undertake to solve through peaceful negotiation all the differences which may arise in the relations between the two countries. They shall negotiate to sign an agreement on the delimitation of the national frontier between the two countries on the basis of the present border line; they are resolved to turn the present border into a border of lasting peace and friendship between the two countries.

Article Five

The two Parties shall fully respect each other's independence and sovereign line.

The two Parties shall pesistently pursue a foreign policy of independence, peace, friendship, cooperation and non-alignment, on the principle of non-interference in any form in other countries' internal affairs, non-acceptance of any interference in their respective countries' internal affairs, and not allowing any country to use their respective countries' territory to interfere in other countries.

The two Parties attach great importance to the long-standing tradition of militant solidarity and fraternal friendship between the Kampuchean, Lao and Vietnamese peoples, and pledge to do their best to strengthen this traditional relationship on the basis of respect for each country's independence, sovereignty and territorial integrity. They shall strengthen their relations in all fields with the socialist countries. Being countries in Southeast Asia, the Socialist Republic of Vietnam and the People's Republic of Kampuchea shall persistently pursue a policy of friendship and good neighbourliness with Thailand and the other countries in Southeast Asia, and actively contribute to peace, stability and prosperity of Southeast Asia. The two Parties shall develop relations of cooperation with the national independent countries, the national liberation movements and democratic movements, and resolutely support the struggle of nations for peace, national independence, democracy and social progress. They shall make positive contributions to the solidarity and growth of the non-aligned movement against imperialism and other international reactionary forces, to gain and defend national independence and to advance towards the establishment of a new world economic order.

Article Six

The two Parties shall frequently exchange views on the questions concerning the relations between their two countries and other international matters of mutual interest. All problems in the relations between the two countries shall be solved through negotiation in the spirit of mutual understanding and respect, and in a way consistent with both reason and sentiment.

Article Seven

The present Treaty is not intended to oppose any third country and does not affect the rights and obligations of each party stemming from the bilateral and multilateral agreements to which it is a signatory.

Article Eight

The present Treaty shall enter into force from the date of the exchange of instruments of ratification; the ratification shall be done according to the procedures of each party.

Article Nine

The present Treaty shall be valid for twenty-five years and thereafter shall be extended by tacit agreement for successive periods of ten years if neither signatory party informs the other in writing one year before the expiry of the Treaty about its intention to cancel the Treaty.

Done in duplicate in the Vietnamese and Khmer languages, both texts being equally authentic, in Phnom Penh, capital of the People's Republic of Kampuchea, on the Eighteenth of February, 1979.

For the Government of
the Socialist Republic
of Vietnam:
[Signed] Pham Van Dong

For the People's Revolutionary
Council of the People's
Republic of Kampuchea
[Signed] Heng Samrin

5
Agreement on Economic Cultural, Scientific and Technological Cooperation between the Lao People's Democratic Republic and the People's Republic of Kampuchea

In order to develop the relations and strengthen the militant solidarity and fraternal friendship between Laos and Kampuchea, and in response to the two countries' aspirations for all-round cooperation and mutual assistance for the cause of building their countries and making them prosperous, the Lao People's Democratic Republic and the People's Republic of Kampuchea have mutually agreed on the following:

Article One

The two sides shall do their best to develop economic, scientific and technological cooperation in conformity with each country's aspirations and legal procedures, based on the principles of respect for independence, sovereignty, equality, mutual benefit, and unreserved mutual assistance.

Article Two

The afore-mentioned cooperation shall cover all spheres: industry, agriculture, forestry, fishing, trade, communications, postal information, culture, education, fine arts, radio broadcasting, television, films, sports, public health, science, technology and other areas.

Article Three

The two sides shall jointly exchange delegations for study tours, visits, and research; exchange experts, teaching and documents; cooperate in research and in training technical cadres and workers; increase the number of meetings and cooperation among the various branches of the state organizations concerned, among mass organizations, and among localities between the two countries.

Article Four

The two sides shall jointly permit and facilitate cooperation in the afore-mentioned spheres.

Article Five

Based on this agreement, all state organizations concerned of the two countries shall jointly agree on the details in protocols determining the contents and form of cooperation for each branch.

Article Six

This agreement shall come into effect on the date of the signing. It shall be valid for five years and will be extended automatically every five years, if neither of the signatories notifies the other in writing of its intention to annul the agreement six months before it is due to expire.

This agreement may be changed and expanded if the two sides jointly agree.

This agreement is concluded in Phnom Penh on the Twenty-Second of March, 1979, in two copies in the Lao and Khmer languages, both copies being equally valid.

For the Lao People's
Democratic Republic:
[Signed] Sanan Soutthichak

For the People's
Republic of Kampuchea:
[Signed] Mok Sakun

INDEX

Afghanistan, 132
ASEAN, 118-21, 123-27, 132, 135-36, 138-51, 153-54, 169

Bandung Conference, 17
Bangkok Post, 109
Barre, Raymond, 59
Battambang, 6
Burma, 147

Chams, 5
Chiang Kai-shek, 175
Chenla I & II, 41n
Chinese Communist Party
  Eleventh Congress, 46
  relations with other parties, 123
  Twelfth Congress, 132
Chinese Empire, 3, 14
Chup-Memot, 68
Coalition government, 124-25, 128, 147, 149, 153, 174
Cochin China, 5, 43
COMECON, 61, 69
Conference of Indochinese Foreign Ministers, 139, 142-43, 146-47, 151
Cuban advisors, 108
Cultural Revolution, 22

Dawee, 118
Democratic Kampuchea, 114, 120, 125, 127-28, 130, 149
Deng Xiaoping, 59, 62, 73, 82, 86-88, 108-10, 118-20, 125
Deng Yingchao, 59

East German advisors, 108
Ethnic Chinese, 45, 48, 60-61, 64, 66, 68, 94, 97, 106, 140, 162-66

Fifth National People's Congress, 59
First Indochina War, 14-15
Fish Hook, 77
France, 3
French Indochina, 3, 7
French-Siamese Treaty, 3

"gang of four", 46
General Prem, 121
Geneva Conference, 15-18
Gia Lam, 69
Guangzhou, 30
Gulf of Tonkin, 40, 110, 155

Han Nianlong, 92, 102, 124
Heng Samrin Regime, 107, 114,

127, 132, 135–36, 138,
141–42, 144–46, 148, 150–51,
168, 173–74
Ho Chi Minh, 8n, 10n, 93
Hoang Tung, 33n, 40, 46, 57n,
74
Hong Kong, 111
Hu Yaobang, 132, 173n
Hua Guofeng, 53–54, 59,
109–10
Huang Hua, 39n, 116, 120
Hyden, William, 129

Ieng Sary, 62–63, 78
India, 147
Indochina federation, 10n,
56–57, 64, 87, 99, 101–2, 105
Indochinese Communist Party,
8, 10
Indochinese People's
Conference, 24
Indochinese states, 143–46, 150,
158, 172, 175
Indochinese Union, 3
Indonesia, 140, 144, 148, 150

Kampuchean Communist Party,
63
Kampuchean National Front for
National Salvation, 77–78
Kampuchean Patriotic and
Democratic Front of Great
Nation, 120
Khieu Samphan, 120, 121–22
Khmer Empire, 2–3, 5, 43
Khmer Rouge, 18, 26n, 29–31,
30n, 31, 33n, 34–36, 38–39,
90, 105–7, 109–10, 113, 117,
119–20, 122, 124, 128, 130,
137, 139, 142–43, 149,

152–53, 156, 161, 165,
167–69, 172, 174–75
Khmers, 5, 8, 30, 33, 35–37, 41
Kissinger, 34n
Kompong Cham, 59, 67, 70, 77
Korean War, 16
Kratie, 67, 77
Kuala Lumpur, 125
Kuantan Principle, 150

Lai Chau, 91
Lao-Kampuchean Agreement,
105
Laos, 4, 7, 10, 15, 19n, 23, 30,
35n, 46–47, 49, 60n, 66, 75,
79–80, 87, 95, 103–5, 107,
114, 138, 143, 145–46, 148,
160, 162, 176–77
Laotians, 8, 9
Le Duan, 47, 54, 174
Le Duc Tho, 34n
Lee Kuan Yew, 121
Li Xiannian, 51–52, 110
Lon Nol, 27–30, 34, 35n, 41n,
43n

Malaysia, 140, 144, 148, 150
Marshal Harin Hongskula, 118
Mekong Delta, 5, 42, 161
Mondale, 111
Mongol embassy, 2n
Mongolia, 132
Moscow, 26, 46–47, 49, 52, 61,
65n, 68, 83, 85, 114–15, 130,
132, 162

National Front for the
Liberation of South Vietnam
(NFL), 23–26, 30
National United Front for the

Liberation of Cambodia, 32
New Delhi, 148
New economic zones, 61
Newsweek, 110
Nguyen Co Thach, 140–41, 147,
149–50, 152–53, 175
Nhan Dan, 40, 46, 74, 79
Non-Aligned Conference, 148
North Vietnam, 17, 20, 25–26,
36, 39, 46
North Vietnamese, 20n, 22–23,
26–27, 29–32, 35–36, 39n,
41, 160

Paracels, 40, 110
Paris Ceasefire Agreement,
34–37, 38n
Parrot's Beak, 77
Pathet Lao, 16, 105
Pen Soven, 176
People's Institute of Foreign
Affairs, 86
Pham Van Dong, 15, 24, 42n,
47, 52, 87
Phan Hien, 94, 139, 101n
Philippines, 144
PLA, 119
Pol Pot, 58n, 63, 68n, 76–78,
80, 90, 95, 101, 108–9, 111,
116, 120, 134–36, 154
Pracheachon, 18

Red Guards, 22
Republican China, 3–4

Saigon, 18, 39
Siam, 3, 6
Siemreap, 6
Sihanouk, 17, 19–22, 24–32, 34,
35n, 37, 38n, 41–42, 45,

120–22, 124–25, 128n,
148–49, 158, 173, 177, 178n
Singapore, 124, 139, 148
Sino-Kampuchean Declaration
of Friendship, 17
Sino-Kampuchean Treaty of
Friendship, 19
Sino-Soviet talks, 130, 132
Sino-Vietnamese border, 68, 84,
107, 110–12, 163–64, 174
Sixth National People's
Congress, 132
Son Sann, 121–22, 124, 155,
176–77
South China Sea, 145–46
South China Sea Islands, 40, 44
South Vietnam, 19, 20, 23, 26,
137
South Vietnamese, 18, 20, 33, 35
Southeast Asia, 11, 13–14, 23,
51, 63, 83, 92, 94–95, 97,
101–2, 140, 171
Southeast Asia, 115, 121–23,
127, 132, 138, 157, 167
Soviet bloc, 21, 162
Soviet Union, 16, 36, 39, 46–47,
50, 52, 60, 62, 65, 69, 80,
83, 88–89, 95, 101, 106–8,
114, 131–33, 166–67
Soviet-Vietnamese Treaty, 69,
75–76, 82, 165–66
Spratly Islands, 40
Summit Conference of the
Indochinese Peoples, 30–32
Sunthorn Hongladarom, 109

Tay Ninh, 67, 75
Thailand, 3, 6, 106–7, 109, 112,
118–19, 121–22, 124, 140–43,
145–47, 152–55

Tributary relations, 2, 3, 14
Tripartite conference, 124
Troung Chinh, 47

UN Conference on Kampuchea,
123, 128, 144-45
United Nations (UN), 49n, 87,
113-14, 116, 120-23, 126,
131, 134-35, 138-39, 145,
148-49, 175
United States, 16, 18-19, 21, 23,
29, 31, 35, 143

Viet Cong, 23-24, 27, 39n
Viet Minh, 5, 10, 15-16, 18
Vietnam-Kampuchea Treaty,
79, 87, 137
Vietnam-Laos Treaty, 49-50, 79
Vietnam War, 161
Vietnam Workers' Party, 10, 15
Vietnamese colonization, 105,
176

Vietnamese Communist Party,
47, 67, 174
Vo Nguyen Giap, 47

Waldheim, 110
Warsaw Pact, 47, 69
White Book on Vietnam-China
relations, 136
Woodcock, 86

Xingjiang Autonomous Region,
89

Yuan Dynasty, 1
Yuyiguan (Friendship Gate), 48

Zhang Weilih, 109, 119
Zhao Ziyang, 122-23, 126,
128n, 129, 132, 173
Zhou Daguan, 2n
Zhou Enlai, 16-17, 21, 28, 35n,
59